THE ACTION TAKER'S GUIDE
TO YOUR DOG BUSINESS

Gamechanger testimonials

Raising Sherlock has at times been heart breaking, heart wrenching and the hard days are still hard, but they are becoming rarer and rarer and I'm getting better at handling them, because I found absoluteDogs.

I needed them, I found them, they saved us.

Zoe Swan

While I was scrolling through Facebook, I came across Tom and Lauren from absoluteDogs. I noticed they were a bit different from the others I had seen before. They showed me another way, fun and clever games-based training that I could fit into my busy lifestyle.

Cathy Tse

I met Lauren at a time I was ready for a change and I took the opportunity that was presented to me...and thanks to Lauren I have learned that I am now truly happy as I am doing something I love, that happiness is a choice. Own it, be it, live it, every day.

Michelle Ingham

A heart-to-heart with Lauren while at Super Trainer 2017, gaining permanent residency and joining Pro Dog Trainer were the three things that I needed to push me into taking the leap and starting my own dog training school. And so Progressive Paws was born.

My training school has been running for a year now and it has been the best year of my life so far. I love that I can design my day, I am in control of what I do and how I choose to spend my time. I love the flexibility running my own training school brings. I love that I can share my passion and spread the awesome message that there are far better ways to train. I love the smiles on my students' faces when they are seeing success on their own journeys. Being in charge of my own destiny is where true happiness really lies for me. I love my life. I am never wishing for the weekend or dreading Monday morning. Every day for me is filled with fun, love and laughter.

Kelly Murrell

I love my job. I love enthusing others with my passion for dog training. Teaching weekly classes, regular workshops, veterinary referrals, bespoke behavioural programmes, 121s and caring for dogs has become an everyday occurrence for me and a dream come true.

The throughline is Lauren Langman's support and friendship. Without Tom and Lauren's belief in me, knowledge and 'can do' attitude I would not have succeeded or perhaps even started.

Nikki Thurston

THE ACTION TAKER'S GUIDE TO YOUR DOG BUSINESS

LAUREN LANGMAN

THE CHOIR PRESS

Lauren Langman is a top agility competitor winning at Crufts, Olympia, winning over 22 Championship tickets and representing Team GB at World Championship level. She owns multiple breeds, and trains in all competitive fields.

Lauren has a Law degree and a post graduate diploma in Education. Lauren owns a number of successful businesses including Devon Dogs, Bowerland Cottage Holidays and absoluteDogs. Lauren has also set up her own world class professional dog centre and hydrotherapy, fitness and rehabilitation centre.

As co-founder of the absoluteDogs Pro Dog Trainer programme, Lauren has helped thousands of people through the start-up process and supporting them as they launch their dog businesses.

Lauren is a solution-seeking optimist who believes in finding and embracing opportunities and is proud Mum to Eliza who lights up her world every single day.

First published in the United Kingdom in 2019 by

The Choir Press

ISBN 978-1-78963-059-6

Dedication

To you, Gamechanger.

To all those action takers who've ever struggled to take the first step, who've fallen and gotten back up, who've completed tasks that seemed insurmountable, who've been knocked down and have bounced up, who've had struggles and turned them into strengths, who showed up and stepped up until their dreams became reality.

To the Gamechangers.

Acknowledgements

With love and thanks to my family, friends, team and tribe. You are all Gamechangers. Thank you. Let's do this together!

Quotes

Wherever possible, the accuracy of the quotes used and their attribution has been checked, however in some instances it has not been possible to verify the quote. If the makers of any quotes that have been misattributed or inaccurately presented would kindly notify the publisher or the author of their having been the original author, then the publisher/author will take all reasonable steps to give the correct attribution on any reprinting.

absolute-dogs.com

CONTENTS

absolute-dogs.com

The Gamechanger Manifesto

Here's to the Gamechangers

To the owners that see struggles and turn them into strengths

The solution seekers

The owners that never accept a relationship & dog is lost

To the game players,

The fun makers,

The joy finders,

The owners who inspire rather than force or deprive

To those who when faced with a struggle scream,

'There's a game for that'

Who reach out and grab real life results

& never (never) stop transforming through games

INTRODUCTION

Here's to the Gamechangers

So you think you want to run a dog business? I know so many great people in the world who want more than they currently have, to move beyond what they currently do, who they currently are, to the life of their dreams. With all of the opportunities in life, why haven't you reached the success that you so badly want? Success and your life will start right here. Welcome to the Action Taker's Guide to Your Dog Business, or in fact any business – here's to the Gamechangers.

But first, let me introduce myself. I am Lauren Langman and I am a Gamechanger. Through my various dog businesses, I help people transform their lives every day. I am a dyed-in-the-wool, solution-seeking optimist, and I love nothing more than helping people turn struggles into strengths. So if you have struggled to get out of the starting blocks with your own dog business, then you have come to the right place.

> *Lauren, 'The Other Side' from The Greatest Showman could have been written about you. You help people trade the typical, normal, drudgery for something way more crazy, colourful and fun every single day.*
>
> Nicola Cameron, Gamechanger

(We love a good soundtrack around here, and in particular The Greatest Showman)

Becoming a Gamechanger

Become a Gamechanger. Set a goal that makes you want to jump out of bed in the morning. Wake up and be awesome!

I remember when I was first training. I had great dogs and a fantastic trainer and I was so passionate about my training. I remember I told my trainer that one day I was going to be a big trainer and have my own business. I was going to be a dog trainer of all breeds, all dogs and all owners, I really was. I believed it with all my heart. And she said to me, "Lauren it's complex – it really is. One day you will get it. People and their dogs, they're so much deeper than what you see on the surface. You are barely scratching at the surface."

At the time I thought hard on it, and I truly did not get what she was on about. Complex? What on earth could be complex about people and their beloved dogs?

Today, it is real. Today I get it, I truly do. I get it: people and their dogs, the relationship is complex. There is so much more to it than meets the eye. And really, it is deep.

To be given the very special opportunity to work so closely with people and their dogs in any capacity is special. They are welcoming you, even in a very small way, into their lives, their family and, most importantly, into their world. Now that's very special. People from all walks of life, with growing relationships, broken relationships, damaged relationships; people who are the enlightened, the soul searchers, the joy seekers, the solution finders – the happy-go-lucky university student, the bullied child, the disheartened ex-spouse, the competitor, the family member, the mother who no longer has her children at home...people come for so many different reasons and from all sorts of places emotionally. You are likely never to know the true reasons behind why they come, but always be aware. Some will come for no reason other than simply to train their dog, but for others, it is so much more.

With this in mind, be kind, be gracious, be grounded, be enlightening, be energetic, be innovative and informative, and always, always, always be grateful to be given this privilege and to have this very special opportunity.

The Gamechanger's way

Are you ready for this? I will share what I have learned about dog businesses, and so much more, and I will share with you the biggest areas of learning that will take you and your dog business to the next level. This book will develop you as an entrepreneur and will prompt you to take the action steps necessary either to start or develop your dog business.

The most important learning point of all is this:

Never, ever stop learning.

The world is a playground and we are all here to learn. Life will give us opportunities to expand our knowledge and understanding every day, and it is so, so important to take every learning opportunity that comes your way.

That said, it is also super important to remember this:

> *Knowledge is not power. Knowledge is only potential power. Action is power.*
>
> Tony Robbins

This book has the potential to change your life. But in order for it to do so, one further piece of the puzzle is needed. And that is ACTION. So I'll need you to do something, and that is to commit. Commit to not just reading this book, but to playing it all out. Do the tasks, take the steps. Learn, then do. It is the only way to progress. It is the Gamechanger's way.

More than a job

I have had a number of businesses myself and I'm going to share with you what I feel is a great mix of recipes for high performance. All of my own businesses have been highly successful and all have links with the dog world in some way or another, from dog training to personal coaching, online coaching groups to seminars abroad, holiday cottages and bespoke programmes to specialist dog training packages. I have also coached, advised, recommended, enabled and mentored hundreds of other businesses, mostly linked in some way to dogs. It excites me, it inspires me and it allows me to keep the fire inside burning so very brightly.

When partnering, coaching and helping someone else to achieve their dreams and passion and grow beyond their wildest expectations, I know my work is so much more than a job. I'm going to share with you some of the very top things that have helped to enable and allow all of those individual businesses to be continually successful. After all, I know that's exactly the kind of business idea you are here for.

This book is going to challenge how you think and supercharge your understanding of just who you are, what is your powerful why and ask you some deeper questions about what exactly it is that you want. Being an action taker, a Gamechanger, is a way of life. In fact, it is a way of survival, and it comes with its very own life toolkit.

You've already taken the first step to becoming a Gamechanger

You have taken action by not only getting hold of your very own copy of the Action Taker's Guide to Your Dog Business, but to actually take that next super vital key step, the step that so very many want-to-be action takers miss, you have physically opened it and are diving in. Now that's real action taking. Congratulations on taking that step. Don't underestimate the power of it: so many people don't even get this far.

Stay open, stay present, stay positive and keep a growth mindset. I'm excited for you, I truly am. Your new life starts here. Fasten your seat belts, this is going to be an amazing ride.

So here's to the Gamechangers

Here's to the Gamechangers

To the owners that see struggles and turn them into strengths

The solution seekers

The optimism bringers

The owners that never accept a relationship and dog are lost

To the game players

The fun makers

The joy finders

The owners who inspire rather than force or deprive

To those who when faced with a struggle scream 'there's a game for that'.

Who reach out and grab real-life results and never (never) stop transforming through games.

Are you ready to be a Gamechanger?

Let's begin. . .

CHAPTER 1

TO THE OWNERS THAT SEE STRUGGLES AND TURN THEM INTO STRENGTHS

If you can see your path laid out in front of you step by step, you know it's not your path. Your own path you make with every step you take. That's why it's your path.

Joseph Campbell

Finding your path

I have always, since I can remember, been involved in dog businesses. They have had complete control of my entire mind, my ultimate success, my days and essentially my life for many years. Along the way I have learned vast amounts, heaps, tonnes, some great and super shareable information to help you get your dog business off the ground and other learning that will help you to find harmony, some balance, a little more authenticity and maybe even more about yourself and who you want to be in the world amongst the complete chaos that can be running any business, let alone a dog business.

Britain's next top lawyer: the original dream

I really wasn't always destined for a dog business career. Really and truly I wasn't . . . or at least not from my family's perspective. I read law at university. I was going to be a top lawyer. In my university days, society and my family were fairly adamant that that was going to be a very positive, prestigious and lucrative direction for me.

I have been lucky enough to be surrounded by some brilliant people my whole life, my family included, who have insisted that at the end of it all, we must follow our passion and our dreams and focus on improving ourselves and challenge ourselves to the deepest level. But it hasn't always been plain sailing. Far from it.

So where did it all really start? I started out with the big dream of being a super successful lawyer, a top barrister. I was going to be great at it. I naively had it all well mapped out in my young mind. Society had helped me with that, society had deemed being a lawyer as 'successful'.

For me it was a thing, the real deal. You want to know why, the real reason behind it? Actually, I knew very little about the legal world or in fact anything to do with law at all. I didn't even watch television to be impressed by how it was portrayed, and I will tell you that my decision making here was pretty poor.

Hard work pays off

I will let you in on a fairly vulnerable secret. After all, we are at our best, we are our most authentic selves when we are truly vulnerable. Vulnerability is a very honourable part of being human. It all started when I was just nine years young. I had a very affluent friend who seemingly had everything I ever wanted. In fact, she had everything that most little girls would ever desire: ponies, a house surrounded by the countryside, dogs, puppies, riding and a truly beautiful life, and her daddy was a very, very successful lawyer.

That was it. My mind was made up. I was going to be a very, very successful lawyer, just like him, and I was going to create that dream, that life. I had that vision. The image was strong, powerful, the desire was great – the powerful why maybe a little flawed for sure. Shallow, yes, that I now know, but at the time it was very real for me all the same and I remember it vividly.

The dream was real and the dream was bright. The desire was supercharged, the vision was clear, the need was super high for that outcome, but the process and the journey were maybe a just a fraction unclear.

I worked hard. I knew the end goal. I was inspired to achieve it. I moved purposefully and I worked diligently. I was going to be a very successful lawyer. I was 11 years old. I gained a place in an all girls grammar school, the Plymouth High School for girls. It was prestigious and I had just barely managed to scrape by with a border-line pass. I worked very hard. I dreamed big. I had a driving force and I was going somewhere. I had my clear vision.

When I left school at 18, I was the highest achieving student, reaching all A grades at A level and receiving merit awards. I was the top-placed student of the year at the ceremony, and I was off university to study law. I was diligently and persistently pursuing my dreams. I had reached the heights and was ready to reap the rewards. Or so I thought.

Finding me

They say that university is a place to find yourself, the place where your new life begins. And for me, that most certainly was true. However, it did not unfold quite as I had envisaged. I hit the ground with a bump pretty quickly. I hit a huge road block, and I mean huge. I really did not enjoy law or studying it in this way, and I realised, at first only quietly to myself, that although I was exceptionally able in the learning department and I had an aptitude for the law, there was actually no way on earth I ever wanted to be a lawyer. Nothing about it really deep down had significance for me. There was no true passion, no true connection. London and city life really weren't for me.

This was a big realisation. At first I didn't know what to do and how to move forward. The feelings were all there, and they were deep rooted: to be true to myself, being a lawyer wasn't me. The real question, though, was – what was? Who was I? And what was I about? I'm sure you have all been here at some point. Maybe you are here right now – maybe that's the reason you are here with me now.

I missed dogs. They occupied most of my brain, 24/7. Dogs were my passion, and they always had been. I just hadn't allowed myself the freedom to consider this and own it. By being enslaved to popular opinion and to society's expectations, I had pretty much signed myself up to a lifetime of boredom.

It was a huge thing to watch the walls of my expectations for my future self, and the dream that I had held from such a young age, crumble. But I knew that being a lawyer wasn't for me and that I had to let it go. I dug deep. I found solace in gratitude and I started to open my eyes to other opportunities. I fell deeply in love with the idea of becoming better and the idea of making great progress, even if I was not yet completely clear on the end purpose. I opened my mind to the concept of growth mindset.

Becoming me

I studied hard. I worked on my law degree. I tried to find, deep inside myself, something I could focus on, and I dug deep. Although I didn't enjoy my degree, I did enjoy the lifestyle, the fun, the energy, the learning process. I fell in love with the library, late nights when I could be alone and tranquil. I loved those nights spent studying. I got so wrapped up in the process of learning that I stuck it out and I played the long-term game for my degree, because the journey and working out the process were more important to me than the outcome. I knew I had something deeper within me – it was brewing – but I also saw how my degree was giving me a whole new world. I just had to work out how I was going to tell my parents.

I worked on my energy. I made good of a bad situation. I am after all an optimist. I made some great energetic connections and friends, and I also made a very important discovery: with the force of great minds, we can make anything happen. *Anything.* Since that day, I have learned that energy and state of mind are so very critical in life, it's key. You have to change the state sometimes to get the desired outcome. Emotion and state change lives. When we change our energy and state, our wiring changes and the way we function changes.

The question is what is really driving you and are you pursuing it? What lights your fire? What is your passion? I worked three jobs, I continued my degree, I graduated and I made some super cool friends. And then I also made some new goals along the way.

> *After that first trip, I started training with Lauren online through the Training Academy and another trip to Devon followed. During this time, I found a new passion, dog training and I started taking a closer look at my life: Was I happy? Did I really enjoy what I was doing?*
>
> Michelle Ingham, Gamechanger

ACTION TAKER TASK: The honesty planner

WHAT YOU DO YOUR LIFE NOW	**WHO YOU ARE** YOUR DREAM LIFE	**YOUR TRANSFORMATION** ACTION TAKING
YOUR CURRENT PROFESSION:	YOUR DREAM PROFESSION:	YOUR VALUES:

LOW **How does it make you feel** HIGH — LOW **How would it make you feel** HIGH

WHAT YOU DO (YOUR LIFE NOW):
- PASSION — 1 ... 10
- ENERGY - Are you energised by what you do? — 1 ... 10
- DO YOU FEEL ALIVE? — 1 ... 10
- DO YOU MAKE A DIFFERENCE — 1 ... 10
- ARE YOU HAPPY? — 1 ... 10
- ARE YOU FULFILLED? — 1 ... 10
- DO YOU DESIGN YOUR OWN DAY? — 1 ... 10
- DO YOU FEEL YOU HAVE MORE TO GIVE? — 1 ... 10
- DOES YOUR WORLD RUN YOU? — 1 ... 10

WHO YOU ARE (YOUR DREAM LIFE):
- PASSION — 1 ... 10
- ENERGY - Are you energised by what you do? — 1 ... 10
- DO YOU FEEL ALIVE? — 1 ... 10
- DO YOU MAKE A DIFFERENCE — 1 ... 10
- ARE YOU HAPPY? — 1 ... 10
- ARE YOU FULFILLED? — 1 ... 10
- DO YOU DESIGN YOUR OWN DAY? — 1 ... 10
- DO YOU FEEL YOU HAVE MORE TO GIVE? — 1 ... 10
- DOES YOUR WORLD RUN YOU? — 1 ... 10

YOUR POWERFUL WHY:

ACTION STEPS YOU CAN TAKE NOW
- ☐
- ☐
- ☐
- ☐
- ☐
- ☐

OBSTACLE WHAT'S STOPPING YOU?	**SOLUTION** OVERCOMING YOUR OBSTACLES	**CREATE YOUR OPPORTUNITY**
		DOING:
		CREATING:
		CHANGING:
		MAKING AN IMPACT WITH:
		My Passion & Dream is...

Come alive

Don't ask what the world needs. Ask what makes you come alive, and go do it. Because what the world needs is people who have come alive.

Howard Thurman

This is how I feel when I'm creating my own path. I'm alive; I'm on fire; I'm working in a higher league. Everything is possible. Because it is.

Which brings us back to the whole purpose of our journey together. You like the idea of a dog business? You love dogs, love people, have skills to share and feel in your heart that a dog business is where your future lies.

You can make it happen.

The age of opportunity is here

The good news is that the traditional barriers to entry in business are gone. Launching a business has never been easier. The need for costly premises and massive marketing budgets has been massively reduced and in some cases eradicated completely as social media allows business owners to reach and speak to their target audiences directly. There is no longer a layer of intermediaries between business and customer.

There are so many opportunities waiting to be explored, and for sure everything is possible right now. Whether it be dog walking, hydrotherapy, physiotherapy and rehabilitation, vet work, behaviour, vet nursing, or whether it is working with dog products and in sales, designing dog items, working online with dogs and their owners, writing, or whether it is puppy rearing, kennels and live-in boarding and home training, lecturing, rescue work, general pet training, day care, grooming, house sitting, sports specific dog training ... you name it, the opportunities are all out there, ready for the making, the taking, the remodelling and reworking, and the redesigning.

And if the particular opportunity you want does not yet exist? Create it.

Make your own lane. These days, there is no need to wait for someone to offer you an opportunity or to wait at home for the phone to ring. Take action. Make it happen.

> *There is no greater gift you can give or receive than to honour your calling. It's why you were born. And how you become most truly alive.*
>
> Oprah Winfrey

ACTION TAKER TASK: What excites you in the dog or business world?

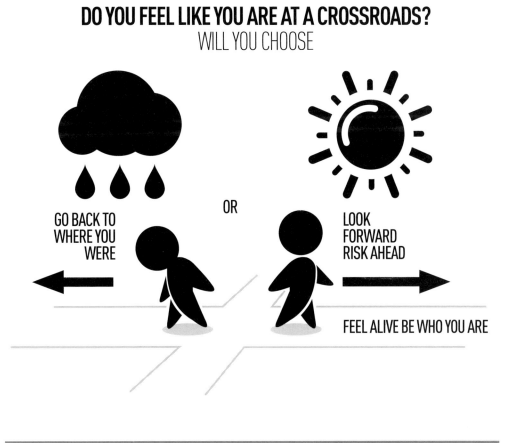

DO YOU FEEL LIKE YOU ARE AT A CROSSROADS?
WILL YOU CHOOSE

GO BACK TO WHERE YOU WERE

OR

LOOK FORWARD RISK AHEAD

FEEL ALIVE BE WHO YOU ARE

Becoming you

*If we did all the things we are capable of, we would literally
astound ourselves.*

Thomas Edison

Before we dive deep and really get stuck in, I do have to ask you a few questions, as I'm really hoping you get it, I mean really get it deep within. The
Action Taker's Guide is about so much more than dog training on every single
level – let me repeat that: this is about *so* much more than dog training or any
dog business. This is not just another book telling you about X, Y and Z and it
is way more than a map from A to B. Are you ready?

*I clung to my planned career like I was drowning. I had
planned to be a veterinarian since I was a child and I
couldn't let it go.*

Megan Moore, Gamechanger

So let me start by asking you those questions. Breathe, dig deep, get gritty,
open yourself up to vulnerability, and be truly honest with yourself.

Are you happy? Right now, how are you feeling? Are you fulfilled by what you
do? Are you doing what you want? Do you design your days? Are you in a
period of uncertainty? Do you know your way? Are you lost a little some days?
Do you doubt yourself? Are you struggling to keep up? Do you contribute? Is
life a race? Do you lack motivation, energy, time? Are you missing your map to
life? Are you feeling like you are falling short? Are you at a crossroads? Maybe
you feel that you could do more? Are you run by the world rather than making
your own decisions? Do you wonder how to move forward, risk ahead and
make a difference?

If any of this resonates with you, then for sure you are in just the right place.
That's exactly where I was, and also where most of our Pro Dog Trainer
students once started. This action taker's guide has taken thousands of
students through this exact process.

And this is where I think my biggest learning curve has been on this whole journey – take action, don't overthink everything!

For months I had been making stories in my own head about how bad the response was going to be from my parents, how disappointed they would be that I wanted to be 'only' a dog trainer.

What was mum's response? "That sounds like an amazing idea, I can hear in your voice how passionate you are about this."

Montana Mays, Gamechanger

The defining factor

It is easy to be negative when you are just starting out and success and fulfilment seem so far away. It is easy to look around at those who have made it already and feel dismayed, to give yourself reasons why you'll never be able to do as they have done, to list advantages they had that you don't have. But I want to let you into a secret:

The defining factor is never resources. It's resourcefulness.

Turn that struggle into a strength.

The ability to find a way, no matter what circumstances present themselves, no matter what obstacle you face, is what will determine how far you go. You are only as good – and will only be as successful – as the toughest obstacle you can overcome. And the confidence you will develop in overcoming each and every impediment will make you unstoppable.

More than a business book

So this project that we are about to embark on, it is a 'project better', a 'project happiness', a project of fulfilment and progress. I think you have realised already that it's about way more than just business. It is so much bigger than that. It is about designing your day, determining your life, finding yourself, contributing more, exploring solution-based thinking, thinking in terms of growth mindset, being your true authentic self, being real, being vulnerable, and enjoying the whole process and experiences and opportunities. Are you in? Are you ready to play all out? Are you ready to not just turn up but show up? Can I get a 'hell, yeah!'?

Find time

Let's do this! Let's take the next, crucial steps to make your move.

But first, some homework. . .

ACTION TAKER TASK: Find time

TIME	SCHEDULE		ADDITIONAL TIME		TIME	YOUR NEW SCHEDULE
07:00	SLEEP				07:00	SHOWER/BREAKFAST
08:00	★ SHOWER/BREAKFAST		1		08:00	PERSONAL DEVELOPMENT
09:00	★ DRIVE TO WORK		1		09:00	COMMUTE & PODCAST
10:00	WORK				10:00	WORK
11:00	WORK				11:00	WORK
12:00	WORK				12:00	WORK
13:00	LUNCH				13:00	LUNCH – RE-ENERGISE
14:00	WORK				14:00	WORK
15:00	WORK				15:00	WORK
16:00	WORK				16:00	WORK
17:00	★ DRIVE HOME		1		17:00	COMMUTE & AUDIO LESSON
18:00	DINNER				18:00	DINNER
19:00	★ TV		1		19:00	EXERCISE
20:00	★ SOCIAL MEDIA		1		20:00	PERSONAL DEVELOPMENT
21:00	★ TV		1		21:00	SOCIAL MEDIA
22:00	TV				22:00	TV
23:00	SLEEP		SLEEP		23:00	SLEEP
00:00	SLEEP		SLEEP		00:00	SLEEP
01:00	SLEEP		SLEEP		01:00	SLEEP
02:00	SLEEP		SLEEP		02:00	SLEEP
03:00	SLEEP		SLEEP		03:00	SLEEP
04:00	SLEEP		SLEEP		04:00	SLEEP
05:00	SLEEP		SLEEP		05:00	SLEEP
06:00	SLEEP		SLEEP		06:00	SLEEP
	TOTAL DAILY TIME		6 HOURS			
	TOTAL WEEKLY TIME		48 HOURS			

★ = Time I can work on my business

absolute-dogs.com

FIND TIME
NOW IT'S YOUR TURN

TIME	SCHEDULE	ADDITIONAL TIME		YOUR NEW SCHEDULE
07:00			07:00	
08:00			08:00	
09:00			09:00	
10:00			10:00	
11:00			11:00	
12:00			12:00	
13:00			13:00	
14:00			14:00	
15:00			15:00	
16:00			16:00	
17:00			17:00	
18:00			18:00	
19:00			19:00	
20:00			20:00	
21:00			21:00	
22:00			22:00	
23:00			23:00	
00:00			00:00	
01:00			01:00	
02:00			02:00	
03:00			03:00	
04:00			04:00	
05:00			05:00	
06:00			06:00	

TOTAL DAILY TIME

TOTAL WEEKLY TIME

IN EACH BOX WRITE <u>ONE</u> THING YOU NEED TO DO NEXT TO REACH YOUR GOAL

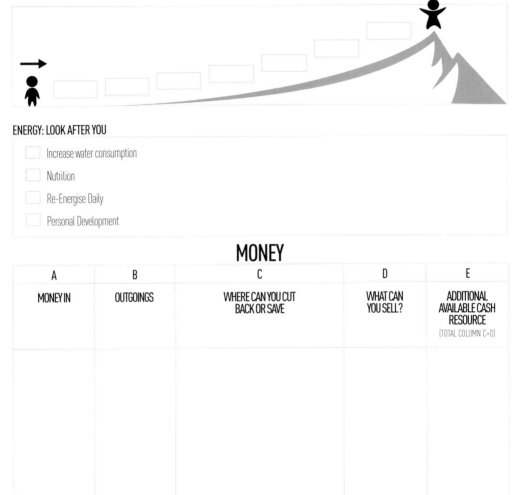

ENERGY: LOOK AFTER YOU

- [ ] Increase water consumption
- [ ] Nutrition
- [ ] Re-Energise Daily
- [ ] Personal Development

MONEY

A	B	C	D	E
MONEY IN	OUTGOINGS	WHERE CAN YOU CUT BACK OR SAVE	WHAT CAN YOU SELL?	ADDITIONAL AVAILABLE CASH RESOURCE (TOTAL COLUMN C+D)

Your powerful why

If you had one piece of advice to someone just starting out, what would it be?

Powerful WHY! Definitely really make sure you have true clarity on this one as you will need to revisit it for an infinite number of reasons!

Claire Warden, Gamechanger

At times on the entrepreneurial journey, things will get tough. When sales are slow, you are completing your tax returns or a client is proving particularly difficult, it is helpful to recall just what prompted you to step into this crazy business world in the first place.

Everyone has their own individual powerful why. There is no wrong, or even right, answer. This is personal, and it's as deep as you want to make it – and it's key to developing your dog business because the single biggest thing that's missing from most people's work is *passion* and a powerful *why*. Enthusiasm and passion will power you forward every single time.

What I have found to be true is that we only really work at our best level, communicate at our best level, perform at our best level, and train at our best level when our powerful why is at the forefront of our minds. It is our driver, our passion, our mission.

So as we set off, let us capture your powerful why.

ACTION TAKER TASK: Your powerful why

1. Write down all of the emotions that you feel right now that relate to developing yourself, who you are and your dog business.

2. Write down, even just a few sentences, describing what life is going to be like when you pursue and achieve what you want to achieve. This may be in three months, six months, maybe a year or even two. How are you going to feel and what is life going to be like in the future?

3. Sum up your powerful why in one sentence.

Now that you have written this down, let's make this real. Keep it somewhere safe, somewhere you can easily refer back to it. When things get tough, this is going to remind you to come back to your passion. It's going to stay at the forefront of your mind. It will supercharge your learning. It will help you through the dark days and the days when you lose focus, and you need to remember why you are doing what you are doing.

Believe in your powerful why – if it comes from the heart, you have the momentum to overcome all obstacles.

Philippa Sjoberg, Gamechanger

ACTION TAKER TASK: Find your powerful why

POWERFUL WHY

HOW DOES YOUR VISION OF YOUR FUTURE MAKE YOU FEEL?.....

DESCRIBE WHAT YOUR LIFE WILL LOOK LIKE.....

4 POWERFUL POSTCARDS + ENVELOPES

MY POWERFUL WHY	IMAGE

☐ COMPLETE ALL 4

☐ ADDRESS TO YOURSELF

☐ GIVE TO A CLOSE FRIEND

☐ ASK THEM TO POST OVER THE NEXT
6 MONTHS AT RANDOM TIMES

Values

Let what you truly value guide you – or be driven by the hustle and bustle of life, the demands of others and the vagaries of circumstance. The choice is yours.

Anonymous

Standing alongside your powerful why are your values. Your values are the things that are important to you. From learning, to making money, to serving the community, to making a difference, values are different and very personal.

Difficulties occur when people try to live out of alignment with their values. For example, they work in a corporate job for 14 hours a day with a two hour commute, but the thing they value most is spending time with their family. People often ignore their own values in a noble, but ultimately unfulfilling, quest to do what is perceived to be right. But please know this, there is no right and there is no wrong. There are only things that work for you or do not work for you. And if you feel unhappy, disgruntled, tired, unsettled or just generally 'off' then there is a good chance that you are living out of alignment with your values.

It is important to keep your values at the forefront of your mind, so check in with them frequently. They can also change over time as the circumstances of your life change – review them often.

ACTION TAKER TASK: Know your values – really dig deep into what matters most to you

WHO YOU ARE	YOUR TOP 10	✔ ✘ OPPORTUNITY
		☐
		☐
		☐
		☐
		☐
		☐
		☐

What's in a name?

Choosing a name for your business can be one of the top sticking points to getting started. Deciding on the name you want to represent you out there in the big wide world can be tough. We humans attach great emotion to names and choosing the perfect name can really hold up proceedings if you get hung up on it. Sometimes you can procrastinate for so long that someone else already uses the name. Or naming can sometimes be rushed and you are then stuck with something that doesn't quite fit or work as well as it might have if you had taken just a bit more time over it. It is all about striking that balance between adequate consideration and keeping things moving.

Here are a few tips on naming:

- Don't use something attached only to your name unless you plan to link it solely to you.

- Try to pick a name that can change locations.

- Try to be unique.

- Leave opportunities for expansion.

Don't let naming hold you back. Get working on the business. Sometimes the perfect name will reveal itself to you as you begin to work.

Devon Dogs in Devon

My two main companies are Devon Dogs and absoluteDogs (co-owned with Matt and Tom). Both allow for all sorts of development, but for sure it would be harder to franchise or grow the Devon Dogs brand in another location. Yes, it does help to locate what we do, but I would also suggest that it might hinder future possible growth opportunities.

Give it all time to bed in

From naming to branding to logos, banners and set-ups, there are endless prospects and possibilities. I would caution you to start soft by printing some literature and working through some logos. Give it all a little warm-up time, because you never quite know how you will see things in just a month's time. A lot changes, and changes fast, and this adjustment time is important in growing a small business.

CHAPTER 2

HERE'S TO THE SOLUTION SEEKERS

Solution seekers

Know your own mind

> *If you don't like where you are, move. You are not a tree.*
>
> Unknown

There is nothing wrong with staying where you are – if, and only if, you are happy there. If you are content with life and happy with where you are, then that is great. Life is full of Should Monsters who tell you that you Should Want This and you Should Do This and you Should Be This and Should Be Doing That. You do not have to do anything at anyone else's behest. Part of being a Gamechanger is knowing your own mind, knowing what you want in life, and knowing when and how to go for it.

A word of warning

Beware of the comfort zone. Sometimes it is easier when you are not particularly happy where you are because there is direct, in-your-face evidence of a need to change. But what if you are quite happy where you are? Things are nice. Comfortable. Ok. Nothing quite sets your soul on fire, but the bills get paid and everything ticks over nicely.

That is the place you need to watch out for. Life feels nice when the thermostat is set to comfortable. No sudden rises or falls in temperature, moderate, always the same. The human brain loves predictability because it saves energy – if everything stays the same, then your brain doesn't have to think too hard and thus conserves energy.

But nothing amazing ever came from a comfort zone.

Be the thermometer, not the thermostat. Don't stay the same. Make that mercury rise and change the game.

Be grateful

That's not to say that we become all ratty and moany and disgruntled with our current lot. I'm a seeker; I always want to evolve. But I also find joy and gratitude in every day and everything that presents itself daily. Always be grateful for what you have and give thanks for what is to come.

Celebrate your present and all the things that have brought you to this point. Then look forward with grateful eyes to your journey and the changes that will come. See your future, feel it and give thanks for it as though it is already yours. Because, energetically speaking, it is. You have created already in your mind.

Change your mind game to one of gratitude and you will be unstoppable.

Hallmarks of a solution seeker

Are you a solution seeker? What does a solution seeker even look like?

A solution seeker is always

- Looking for answers
- Ready to take an opportunity
- Looking to learn
- Ready to make a connection
- Working in solutions, not problems
- Looking for answers
- Engaging in teamwork
- Is gritty
- Is flexible
- Is optimistic

The solution seeker in the mirror

Some solution seekers are born, some are created. Don't be disheartened if you feel you do not have all these attributes. I suspect that you may have at least some of them, or you would not be reading this book. For those to whom solution seeking does not come naturally, the key to change starts with awareness. Look for opportunities to practice the solution seeker mindset. If your mind defaults to closed, negative thinking, simply acknowledge it and then turn your thoughts around. What would a solution seeker do? How would they look at this situation?

The best bit is that approaching things as a solution seeker feels great. It is the key that opens the doors that negative, closed thinking slams shut.

Growth mindset

> *Chimp: Will I be good at it? It's a huge responsibility! Will I be able to pay all the investment? What if a dog runs away? What if the owners will not understand my Frenchie-English?*
>
> *Me: Go for a dog walking or training course! Be prepared for every situation. Believe in yourself!*
>
> *Chimp: What people will say? "All that studies and work just to become a dog walker!"*
>
> *Me: Don't care! The real questions are: Will I feel fulfilled? Will my family and I be happy? Will I be a good example for my kids? And the responses to all those questions were YES!*
>
> Raoudha Macros, Gamechanger

What is a growth mindset?

A growth mindset is vital to being a solution seeker. A growth mindset means we believe that our abilities can be developed through dedication, persistence and hard work, and that we can change and evolve. It is the solution seeker's mindset. This view reflects the love of work, the love of learning and the gritty resilience that are essential for great accomplishment.

Cultivate your growth mindset. Always look to grow, expand, develop, imagine, create, build.

Having a deep-rooted growth mindset for life will keep you moving forward so you achieve your dreams. Children generally have growth mindsets. They live in a world of colour, rather than the black and white adult world. Throw off the shackles of having to get the 'right' answer or to 'get it right first time'. Try, fail, learn and try again. This isn't Millennial Snowflakery, where you mustn't say that someone is wrong. It is iteration in a growth mindset and it is impossible to achieve anything without it.

This is *big*. Growth mindset is everything. It's a mindset of knowing things won't always go well, someone might steal your idea, people won't always be nice to you, you may fail – but you will always make your way back to the drawing board, review, revise, plan and try again.

Remember, the master has failed more times than the beginner has ever tried.

No one is an island

Surround yourself with growth mindsets whenever and wherever you can. Look for the people, the books, the online content, anything that helps you to expand your mind and develop growth thinking. Push harder, push your mindset and surround yourself with people who push you.

Opportunity is everywhere

The very best bit about this is that the world is crying out for solution seekers. The very essence of business is to solve problems. If you can solve a problem and can charge for doing so, then you have the basis for a business. Opportunity really is everywhere for the solution seeker.

Solution seekers will spot the huge variety and opportunity within the dog world. Gone are the days when you had to wait for a job advert to invite you to join the world of dog-related business. There are so many chances to mix things up, to change what's written, to adapt to your own beat, to play your own song and to always, always take every single opportunity that comes your way or strikes your fancy.

Never say no to learning. Look for opportunities around every corner. Keep your eyes peeled for novelty and inspiration and always be hungry for more. Be hungry for change. Be the change that you are looking for.

Look out for amazing opportunities in all directions so that you are ready to say yes any moment it is offered up to you. Then you will be ready to spot the opportunity as it arises and grab it before it's too late. Learn to make well-considered decisions quickly – and always, always take action. If you don't, someone else will.

Life's opportunities present a bit like the conveyor belt at one of those sushi restaurants: the opportunity will present itself in the moment. It is up to you to choose your plate, and those dishes that you don't grab will drift away. Some might come back again, some might be taken by others, some might be replaced. Decisiveness is key.

And if there isn't an opportunity – make one

And what if life does not serve up the dish you want most? Well then, just get in the kitchen and make it yourself. We live in a world where accessing market-places and customers has never been easier. Global business reach is accessible to someone sitting at their kitchen table. Know your skills and be creative in how you apply them to the dog world.

We hear so many people say the words, 'I would love to do that, but...' and with that 'but' they put themselves back into a box, shelve their dreams and leave the world of dog business to the 'lucky ones'. It is sad because it doesn't have to be that way.

Dog ownership today is massive. There is a huge worldwide market. You do not have to wait for someone to offer you an opportunity. Be bold. Leverage your talents and skills, find a way to apply them to the dog world, and become part of that world.

Our ProDog Trainer programme is the perfect place to start. ProDog Trainer is a step-by-step, zero to hero course on becoming a professional dog trainer. Covering all aspects of delivering games based concept training, it will arm you with the tools you need to go confidently out into the dog world as a trainer.

Don't wait to be picked to be one of the lucky ones. Make yourself one of them.

Solution seeking superheroes

If you are in a tight spot, you want a superhero around, right? Someone clad in Lycra with all the ideas and ability to get you out of a jam? Of course.

But what if I told you that you don't need to be clad in Lycra to be a solution seeking superhero? The power lies within you to be that person who comes up with the creative solution and implements it, who sees a problem and overcomes it, who always has the way to save the day. It is so, so possible.

The superhero journey

Of course, every good superhero story needs a journey. Having a solution – no matter the situation I find myself in is a hugely comforting place to be. Personally for me, whether I'm feeling stuck, nervous, overwhelmed, anxious, stressed out, exhausted, out of control or conflicted, I'm certain I can always come up with a solution these days. The solution is like my medicine and it's a mindset change. It's a way of life and it becomes a beacon of bright light in each and every day.

Unleashing your superpower

Success is achievable if you collect the right tried-and-tested beliefs and habits. If you have the right beliefs and habits, and surround yourself with the right people, and grow the right energy around you, then success is the natural result. It's a force, and it's unstoppable. It really is a force of nature.

And this isn't just me, for each one of the many lives transformed through our ProDog Trainer Online Programme the tipping point to success on their superhero journeys is that moment they adopted the solution seeker mindset – the superpower everyone has capacity for.

Remember too that almost all superheroes have imperfections, walking flaws, foibles, shortcomings. Remember, you don't succeed because you have no flaws or weaknesses: you are human. You succeed because you find your special unique strengths and you focus them, you target them, you home in on them and you grow them, and you then develop habits around those strengths.

Everyone has tough days. Everyone has flaws and weaknesses. Don't focus on those. Where you focus your energy is where your energy goes. Everyone is fighting their own battle, and it's a battle you know nothing about. Everyone has their struggles. It is how you come through them and overcome them that counts.

Superheroes do what the average person does not do: they go on despite their flaws. They take their struggles and turn them into strengths, and they always, always have a solution to a difficulty. Become a superhero. Don't let your flaws hold you back. Seek to transform your struggles into strengths, and cultivate your solution seeking abilities. Life will throw curveballs at you, but with these superpowers, you will triumph.

What if I fall?

Oh, but my darling, what if you fly?

Erin Hanson

ACTION TAKER TASK: Are you a solution seeking superhero?

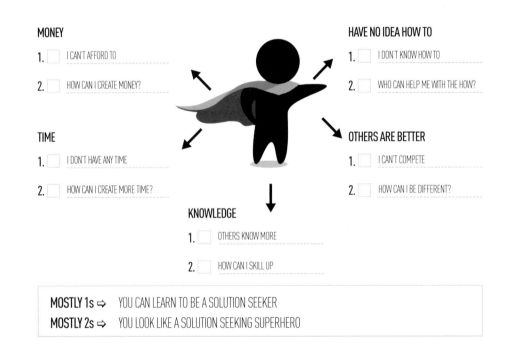

MONEY
1. ☐ I CAN'T AFFORD TO
2. ☐ HOW CAN I CREATE MONEY?

TIME
1. ☐ I DON'T HAVE ANY TIME
2. ☐ HOW CAN I CREATE MORE TIME?

HAVE NO IDEA HOW TO
1. ☐ I DON'T KNOW HOW TO
2. ☐ WHO CAN HELP ME WITH THE HOW?

OTHERS ARE BETTER
1. ☐ I CAN'T COMPETE
2. ☐ HOW CAN I BE DIFFERENT?

KNOWLEDGE
1. ☐ OTHERS KNOW MORE
2. ☐ HOW CAN I SKILL UP

MOSTLY 1s ⇨ YOU CAN LEARN TO BE A SOLUTION SEEKER
MOSTLY 2s ⇨ YOU LOOK LIKE A SOLUTION SEEKING SUPERHERO

Becoming a solution seeker

Before, if I was ever faced with a struggle, I would only see the problems and I dreaded tackling it. Now, if there is a problem, be it dog training, relationships, work – I now think solutions! It's an amazing feeling to know that you can face any challenge as a positive and an opportunity to grow.

Lucy Full, Gamechanger

Stay open

Always, always continue to grow, improve and develop. Never stop learning. Stay grounded and stay humble to learning. I have learned that I still have so much more to learn. Stay curious, always, about what you do. Stay open, playful and inquisitive, for being so will drive you in the direction of your goals, your dreams and your ultimate desires, pleasure and happiness.

ACTION TAKER TASK: Make notes – where do I want to grow? What do I want to learn next? What is my next area for growth?

We are students for life and we are students of life. We always grow, always evolve, remodel, tweak it, change it up, develop and keep learning, always keep learning.

Push yourself – it's always worth it.

Life has no remote control. You have to get up and change whatever it is you want to change.

Feel the fear and do it anyway

Work on you. The thought of change – changing yourself, changing your situation, changing what you are and what you do – can be scary. Fear can be truly crippling. It is your brain's way of keeping you safe. It literally stops you in your tracks.

The secret is to remain calm. Thank your brain for having your back, but let it know that there is no cause for concern. Yes, you are contemplating something new. Yes, that is different. But no, it is not a threat to your very survival. You will be ok. Chances are you will be better than ok.

Also remember that fear creates the same feelings as excitement. It feels the same to your body and mind. Top athletes and performers feel fear just as we do, but they learn to master the feeling, to reframe it as excitement. They choose to feel excited, not fearful, when those feelings arise. So when your heart rate starts to rise and your palms start to sweat, be grateful for the excitement you are feeling about what are doing and go for it.

Chunk it

If you really struggle with fear, break your task down into the smallest pieces possible. Pick the easiest one and do it until it is complete. When you've completed it, pick the next easiest task and do that. Once you've done a few small tasks, your brain will see that it is not so scary and will call off the alarm bells. You'll build a bit of momentum, which will give you confidence, and you will be able to progress.

Fear is a part of success. Doing new things should scare you a bit: it is a sign you are leaving your comfort zone behind. Channel it, leverage it to move you forward, overcome it. Being scared and still moving forward is bravery and it becomes a muscle, something you flex and get used to using. It gets stronger the more you use it. Success is something that will scare you, enlighten you, freak you out some days, you will have failures, you will come out on the other side more aware. Face your fears, get back up, jump back up, learn the lessons, go valiantly into the storm. If you have fear then that's good, it means it matters to you. Now that's an exciting place to be.

Most of the world is playing it safer than you are. Be brave, be bold!

What you can do, or dream you can, begin it; boldness has genius, power, and magic in it.

John Anster

Keep on keeping on

Never, never, never quit. There's a lot of truth in the oft-repeated "patience, persistence and perspiration are an unbeatable combination for success". You can't beat someone who won't quit. As Will Smith says:

"The only thing that I see that is distinctly different about me is I'm not afraid to die on a treadmill. I will not be outworked, period. You might have more talent than me, you might be smarter than me, you might be sexier than me, you might be all of those things you got it on me in nine categories. But if we get on the treadmill together, there's two things: You're getting off first, or I'm going to die. It's really that simple, right?

You're not going to outwork me. It's such a simple, basic concept. The guy who is willing to hustle the most is going to be the guy that just gets that loose ball. The majority of people who aren't getting the places they want or aren't achieving the things that they want in this business is strictly based on hustle. It's strictly based on being outworked; it's strictly based on missing crucial opportunities. I say all the time if you stay ready, you ain't gotta get ready."

Hard work trumps talent every day of the week. There's a magic in consistency of effort and endeavour. In showing up every day and putting in the work, you are showing the Universe that you want it, and you will find that serendipity, coincidence and kismet all begin to align and assist the tangible results of solid, ongoing effort. Amazing things start to happen when you put your head into the yoke daily.

The tough times

Of course, there will be bumps in the road and days when you just don't feel like it. What do you do then? You just do it. Do it. Do it. Do it. And do it again. And then keep on doing it. You will only ever rise to the level of the toughest obstacle that you cannot overcome. Successful people do what needs to be done, when it needs to be done, whether they feel like doing it or not. And if there isn't a clear path to what needs to be done? They make one.

Value others

Be humble. Always know that someone can share a valuable insight at any moment. Every person you meet has something to teach you. That moment of learning is always happening. That moment is happening right now and will continue to happen for the solution seekers.

Grow

Solution seekers grow all the time. Always ensure you have time in each and every day to grow personally. They say it's better to know how to learn than to know, because when we know how to learn it becomes a habit. It becomes who we are, how we live and how we navigate daily life.

We live in a very permission-based society, where you wait to be told whether you've passed the test, completed the piece of work adequately, won the tender, met your sales target. Being an entrepreneur takes courage, faith in your own ability and the confidence to proceed without waiting for permission. If you know that you can always learn from anything that happens, that knowledge will stand you in very good stead for your entrepreneurial journey.

ACTION TAKER TASK: Plan your transformation – what will help you to grow?

KNOWLEDGE

OPPORTUNITIES

BELIEF

MINDSET

SOLUTION SEEKING SUPERHERO
TRANSFORMATION

FROM THIS

TO THIS

Personal growth for the solution seeker

Here are just a few of our top tips for fully rounded personal growth:

Take an online course or join an online community. For example, we have the ProDog Trainer programme – this incorporates all elements of what you need to get continued growth, momentum and success and a community of likeminded solution seekers to boot! This is effectively the university of dog training and dog business – the superhero stories of those action-takers that have been through it are inspiring in themselves.

The online world is huge, and growing at a crazy speed. If your fixed mindset is baulking at the idea that being online might not be for you, keep an open mind.

Or maybe you are already part of an online group. If so, dive in a bit deeper. There will be something out there for you – you just need to seek it out. Remember, opportunity will rarely knock on your door, looking directly for you. You need to seek it out. Find your tribe, find your energy and love them hard. Who you surround yourself with is who you become. We absorb energy from those we associate with, so be super selective with your guides and mentors.

Never stop learning. Who we associate with, who we spend our days with, what books we read, whose energy we absorb – this all has an impact on us. Often what limits our ability to grow and develop is that we believe that we already know everything. But actually opening up ourselves to learn from the people around us, selectively choosing people around us, opening up our hearts and observing everything can be educational. We should be so very focused on improving ourselves.

Invest in yourself. Spend money on your own personal development. Don't let money be an issue in gaining the knowledge you need to take you to the next level. Make that investment. You need to speculate to accumulate, as they say, and this is a dead cert. If you commit time and resources to self-improvement, you are guaranteed to reap the rewards.

Make new contacts and friends. Talk to people. Tell them about yourself and about your business. Arrange meet-ups at local businesses and share ideas and energy. Energy is so very transferable and it's what makes us and keeps us alive. Stay around great energy. Anyone can be your teacher, so observe closely. Set up a small group of like-minded individuals, meet once a month, stay accountable, seek solutions together, grow together, discuss strategy and work out how you can help each other.

Learn a new skill. Learn something that backs up or adds to what you do. Add on a plus service or learn something new about your current topic to enable you to go that extra mile. For example, this year I have been learning scent, gundog work, and a little search and rescue.

Learning something new is a fantastic way to keep your energy high, your emotions engaged and your motion moving forward – and energy is emotion in motion. Developing your skills is hugely satisfying on every level and is key to becoming an action taker.

Always look out for an opportunity. Shadow an excellent person in your field. Learn from those who have walked before you, and those who walk alongside you. There is no need to reinvent the wheel. The way forward is for sure to model yourself on fantastic mentors and then to add your own creativity as and when it feels right – but relax, and enjoy shadowing the top people in your field, or, for that matter, out of your field.

Modelling successful people and successful thoughts, and learning in the role are the very best ways to grow. Don't follow the broken people who are struggling and can't work out their struggles. Follow the people who truly know how to seek solutions and change, in their own small way, how the world works.

Listen to podcasts. They allow you to learn and grow while travelling, first thing in the morning, last thing before bed, walking your dog, running, you name it. A podcast is a flexible way for you to learn and grow while in motion. It is efficient and it is hugely motivating.

When you think you are working hard, put the hustle in and work a little harder. Yes 10% will make a difference, but how about 25% harder? It is possible – it just needs a minor shift. Get up a little earlier, go to bed a fraction later, cut down your social media time, delegate a task that doesn't need you. Be careful of what you agree to do and what impact doing it will have on your time.

Time is a precious resource – guard it, and use it wisely. By being mindful of what you take on, creative with how you get things done and working just that little bit harder, you will grow, develop and add in those areas you haven't yet even considered.

Be an efficient learner. You are learning and growing right now! You are reading (or listening) to a book, so give yourself a virtual high five. Whoop, reward yourself, because learning and growing feel great. So read a book, order a book, get a digital download or a DVD, watch a video or a TED Talk, and find the pieces that jump out at you.

Focus on the empowering concepts, the important strong words, the key words. Extricate the most fascinating information. You don't have to digest every word: draw out the concepts. We don't really need every word. You will free up more time and grow more knowledge without needing to devote hours of every day to the task, and you will make rapid progress.

Know your strengths and weaknesses. What do you love and what are you good at? All too often we are encouraged by society to improve ourselves by working on our weaknesses, but that is not the way to the top. By all means, learn to manage your weaknesses so that they will not hamper your progress, but remember that there will always be other people out there who can do the things you can't – and will usually be very glad to do so in exchange for payment.

So if figures aren't your thing, do not spend endless hours trying to learn accounting. Hire an accountant. Know and lean in to your strengths. There are only so many hours in the day: do not waste them on trying to improve at something that you will only ever be average at. Your awesomeness needs your attention.

Invest in what you love. Invest in your passions and grow that talent. Passion is everything. It is the most powerful asset you have. So on a practical level, book a live face-to-face course, have a bespoke holiday, indulge a little, have a chance to follow your love, and enjoy and allow yourself time for your passion.

Know that you are here for a reason. You came to this world, at this time, in this body, with these talents, for a reason. Only you can fulfil your mission. No one else has the particular blend of skill set, motivation and ability that you have. You do not serve the world by trying to hide your light. Let it shine.

ACTION TAKER TASK: Complete the following to create an action plan for personal growth

WHO DO YOU SURROUND YOURSELF WITH?

PEOPLE AROUND YOU...

DO THEY MAKE YOU LAUGH? ....

DO THEY SUPPORT YOUR IDEAS? ....

DO THEY ENERGISE YOU? ....

DO THEY INSPIRE YOU? ....

DEVELOPING YOU...

ACTION

ONE BOOK I WILL READ .... ☐ DONE

ONE TED TALK I MUST WATCH .... ☐ DONE

ONE WEBSITE I WILL LOOK AT .... ☐ DONE

3 PODCASTS I WILL LISTEN TO...

.... BY ....

.... BY ....

.... BY ....

EVENTS I WILL ATTEND...

3 PEOPLE TO HELP ME

.... DATE ....

.... DATE ....

.... DATE ....

5 THINGS RELATED TO BUSINESS I'D LIKE TO KNOW MORE ABOUT...	ACTION TAKEN TO MAKE IT HAPPEN
1:	1:
2:	2:
3:	3:
4:	4:
5:	5:

PRIORITISING YOUR TIME

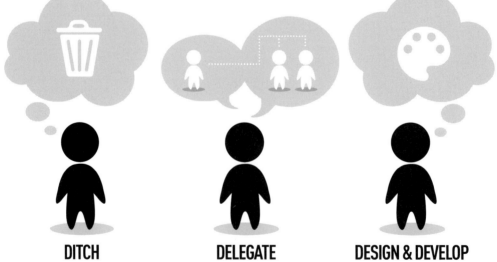

DITCH   **DELEGATE**   **DESIGN & DEVELOP**

MY PASSION IS

TEACHING

I ROCK AT

IDEAS

INNOVATION

PROGRESS

ENERGY

COACHING

MY MISSION IS

BECOMING A DOG TRAINER

I SUCK AT

DESIGN

SOCIAL MEDIA

PHOTOGRAPHY

WRITING

ORGANISING

I ROCK

	THE WHO	COST
IDEAS	ME	TIME
INNOVATION	ME	TIME
PROGRESS	ME	TIME
ENERGY	ME	TIME
COACHING	ME	TIME

THE HOW...I SUCK!!

DESIGN	CRAIG	CASH
SOCIAL MEDIA	TOM	TIME
PHOTOGRAPHY	MEL	COACHING
WRITING	SARAH	COACHING
ORGANISING	MICHELLE	COACHING

MY PASSION IS

....

I ROCK AT

....
....
....
....
....

MY MISSION IS

....

I SUCK AT

....
....
....
....
....

	THE WHO	COST

5 THINGS RELATED TO BUSINESS I'D LIKE TO KNOW MORE ABOUT...	ACTION TAKEN TO MAKE IT HAPPEN
1:	1:
2:	2:
3:	3:
4:	4:
5:	5:

Goal setting for the solution seeker

Goals. There is no telling what you can do when you get inspired by them. There is no telling what you can do when you believe in them. And there is no telling what will happen when you act upon them.

Jim Rohn

Get some goals

Continue to grow and develop for the better. Appreciate the opportunities that you have surrounding you. The future is truly in your hands. Forget about far-off dreams; get passionate about short-term goals. Setting goals will allow you to make huge progress, especially if you commit them to paper and set out to achieve them in whatever format enables you to feel great.

The winning goal setting formula

SMART goals are a huge part of solution-based thinking and they are part of every aspect of human life: how you conduct your relationships, your business, your life; what you want to achieve; the way you use your time. You name it, SMART goals will cover it.

A SMART goal is:

- Specific: set out clearly what you want to improve or achieve – what are you aiming for?

- Measurable: how will you be able to gauge improvement? What will be your measure of success?

- Achievable and attainable: big goals are great, but impossible goals are soul destroying.

- Relevant: it makes sense for you to do this, has a point and improves your life in some way.

- Timely: Put a timescale on it.

Overachievers can add a Y to the acronym to have a SMARTY goal:

- Why: what motivates you?

Write 'em down

Write your SMART goals down and check in with them as often as is necessary to keep them at the forefront of your mind. Review daily or weekly, whatever is appropriate to your timescale.

ACTION TAKER TASK: Go on, get each of those goals written down

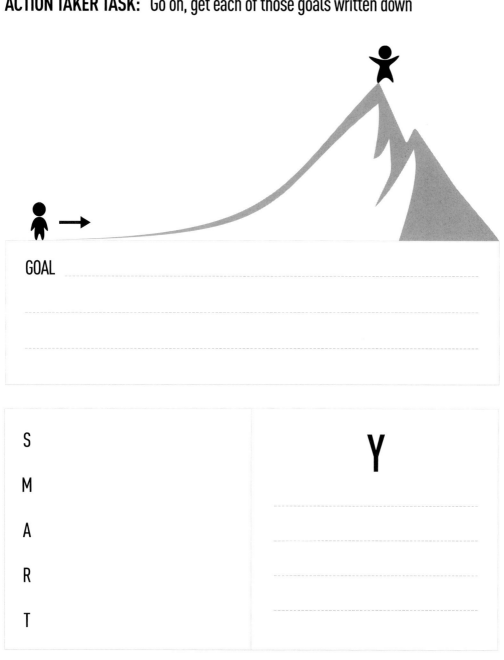

GOAL

S

M

A

R

T

Y

Be accountable

Commit to your goals. Make them public. Tell people what you are aiming to achieve. If you aren't quite up for splashing them all over social media, then tell at least one person close to you what you are doing. Having an account- ability buddy – someone out there who will ask how things are going, especially if that someone will be firm with you and hold you to progress – is a boon on the days when your motivation and energy are flagging.

Celebrate

Resting on your laurels is not exactly something we entrepreneurs are known for. We are usually too busy getting on with the next thing. But achievement is an awesome thing and is to be celebrated. When you hit a goal, celebrate the achievement of it.

Be sure to reward yourself for your effort, even if it is just a pat on the back. Like our dogs, we need reward to keep us going, and although achievement is rewarding in itself, that only really works if you take a moment to acknowl- edge it. Be kind to yourself and be sure to celebrate your wins.

Then set some more

The purpose of a goal is to become something more, something bigger. It is not the goal itself; it is the progress and the growth that are really exciting and will take you to a higher level. Progress is exciting and it's one of the biggest internal drivers out there. When you achieve a goal you only feel good for a short time because the purpose of the goal is to grow – which is why you move to the next goal.

Moving on to the next goal once you have celebrated is essential. After all, it is the process of getting to the goal that brings the joy. Setting the next goal is key.

> *"Would you tell me, please, which way I ought to go from here?"*

> *"That depends a good deal on where you want to get to," said the Cat.*

"I don't much care where –" said Alice.

"Then it doesn't matter which way you go," said the Cat.

From Alice in Wonderland by Lewis Carroll

Common goal fails

Here are some of the very typical and common struggles, frequent downfalls and likely mistakes that people make when they are setting their goals.

1. Are your goals too vague? Are they able to be defined? Be specific about the goals you want to achieve. Be very detailed to make sure you set SMART goals.

2. Are your goals too grand? Are they reachable? Are they pushy but achievable? Bill Gates said people overestimate what they can do in one year but underestimate what they can do in ten years. That's so very true: just pause and think about that for a moment. Think of goal setting like little building blocks that will allow you to bring in change. They will allow that change to happen and make a difference.

3. Goals and influences and the company that you keep all go hand in hand. Are you surrounded and influenced by the right people? Spend time with the people who have the right goals and who have achieved their goals and have made achieving goals a habit. In addition, infuse yourself and your goals with the right energy.

> *For motivation's sake we must be vigilant and surround ourselves with genuine and positive people who seek positive aims with positive attitudes.*
>
> Brendan Burchard

Goal setting makes it possible to plan for future success and will enable you to realise the huge scope of what you do, so you can find your passionate dog business. Create actionable goals that inspire and excite you. Make sure you can see them happen, and that they move you forward. That progress will drive you.

If you aim at nothing, you will hit it every time. Everything – yes, *everything* – is possible. So let's think about the next year: What could be different? Where could your business be? What could you offer that you don't already? Who can help you? How can you action this? Who can lift this off the page?

ACTION TAKER TASK: Here is a place for you to doodle, to dream, to map, to think, to create. Utilise every bit of it. Don't judge or dismiss any of your ideas. Jot them down, capture them, work them through your mind and onto the paper. Tease out the best bits, and start to get them into some order. It is head space – we all need head space.

Dealing with criticism and failure

The biggest barrier was people thinking it was impossible to change a dog just by playing games. Criticism from old-fashioned trainers and dog owners, still stuck on dominance theories. To overcome it, I changed my diet, I became selective and stopped following people who put other people down. I surrounded myself with people who believe it is possible. I found my tribe!

Alexo Gritsipis, Gamechanger

Haters gonna hate

Dealing with criticism or other people's opinions can be a source of stress for so many. Criticism will happen. It is a fact, so being prepared and ready for it makes it all that little bit easier. Let's turn it around, and build some momentum for the solution.

How to handle criticism

1. Listen up. Sometimes there are some really useful points and we can learn from the experience. Constructive criticism for sure has a place.

2. Respond calmly.

3. It's not personal. Take it in the way it's intended – for development.

4. Manage stress.

5. Keep on keeping on – it takes bravery to put your ideas, talents and efforts out there into the world where they can be criticised. Roll with the punches and don't let them stop you moving forward.

What is constructive feedback or criticism?

Offering thoughtful feedback can help us to develop and gain valuable insight into our own actions. It can also help hugely to develop trust, good teams and relationships among staff members.

Try not to be oversensitive to feedback, or you may never get it again. It can be very difficult for people to offer feedback. Considered, thoughtful feedback comes from a place of truth that can be uncomfortable for people to offer, and many people simply will not go there.

Feedback helps you to grow and develop, so try to listen as closely as you possibly can. Be all ears. Try to learn and grow from it instead of being defensive. If you do find yourself becoming defensive, interrupt yourself. Have a band on your wrist or a self-interrupter that will help you to be more openly aware of your response and to manage it.

Thank people for their comments, and be respectful, no matter what the feedback is. Even if you didn't want it or it wasn't what you needed, or it wasn't called for. Be sincere in your thanks. Always remember that feedback makes you better. See it for the opportunity for improvement that it is, and smile.

Don't ever take it personally

This is a tough one. You've poured your heart, resources, time, everything into a product or service, sent it out into the world, and now someone is offering their opinion on just what is wrong with it. That product or service is a reflection of all your efforts. It came from your very soul – it reflects *you* – and it is so hard to accept that any criticism of it is not an attack on you as a person. But, believe me, it is not. It is simply someone else's opinion on how it could work or be a little bit better, and how you could improve it. You may take it on board and make changes, or you may decide to leave things as they are. The choice is always yours.

Having scope for improvement shows that you are out there creating, not stuck in a box dreaming. It does not mean you are fundamentally flawed as a person. Try to remove yourself from the situation and focus on what's being criticised. Take it as a reminder to try a little harder. Focus a little more. Take a little time and skip all of the social media noise and realise we are only human. It's fine to have areas we need to grow in.

This is no time for ease and comfort. It is the time to dare and endure.

Winston Churchill

Don't be judgy

Read more books than status updates. Look into more eyes than screens. Hold more hands than devices. Love more than you judge.

Dulce Ruby

We should be so very focused on improving ourselves and learning that we really and truly don't have energy to criticise anyone else. Judging is critical and observing is educational.

Have the courage to offer feedback where you think it could help, but always make sure it is constructive. We don't want to show people how powerful we are – we want to show them how powerful they are. We want to learn how to empower others.

When we are trying to improve ourselves, we need to surround ourselves with people who challenge us. If you are the smartest person in the room, you need to change the room. Never let compliments go to your head and never let criticism get to your heart. That way you can truly start to build with genuine and authentic learning. Someone can share insight at any moment that can change our lives. We are students for life. When learning becomes a habit, we are on a sure-fire path to success.

The capacity to learn is a gift, the ability to learn is a skill, but the willingness to learn is a choice.

Brian Herbert

Dealing with failure

Success is not final, failure is not fatal: it is the courage to continue that counts.

Winston Churchill

A winner is just a loser who tried one more time

*You won't get it right every time. Don't beat yourself up –
learn from it!*

Caroline Johnson, Gamechanger

Thomas Edison's endeavours to refine the light bulb are frequently spoken of, and while it is hard to pinpoint just how many times he tried, with reports ranging from 1,000 to 10,000 times, one thing for sure is that he tried many, many times and endured many, many unsuccessful attempts before that final breakthrough.

Failure can fill the stress bucket and many people simply cannot tolerate it. Many of us experience setbacks and failures in everyday life. Eventually we get emotionally drained, tired and exhausted. We become unmotivated and we stop trying.

We believe that because we have been unsuccessful in the past that the barrier still exists even for new ventures. We continue to see a barrier in our heads, even though there is no real barrier at all. We have stopped trying only due to our limited beliefs. That barrier is separating us from our dreams. You only fail when you stop trying.

*Our greatest weakness lies in giving up. The most certain way
to succeed is always to try just one more time.*

Thomas Edison

CHAPTER 3

THE OPTIMISM BRINGERS

The optimism bringers

Who is your team? How does your team work? Team work is about so much more than just working together with others to achieve a goal. Team work is about finding and attracting the optimism bringers, the shape shifters, the joy finders and the light bringers. It is about being part of the right groups and creating the groups, being in the right mindset and knowing the optimism bringers in *your* world.

The value of an awesome team and leadership of an amazing group of people is unexplainable. It's massive, and so much bigger than anything I can clearly put into words. These are the people around you who help, support and allow so much to grow within you. Family, friends, connections and being part of a wider team all help to keep us in check, keeps us balanced and allows us to be *real*. No one person is an island. For our Pro Dog Trainers, team really is crucial.

The impact of the individual on the individual

Energy is everything. The way you experience life is totally a question of mindset. Two people can look at the exact same set of circumstances and have two very different experiences of them. You can't choose what happens to you, but you can choose how you react to it. Optimism is always the best way. Down the pessimism road lies disheartening, closed thinking and an inability to overcome obstacles. There is no such thing as an obstacle or failure to an optimist. Everything is an opportunity to learn and to try harder. Guard your own mindset. If things are tough and you find your optimism wavering, stop for a moment, take a deep breath and look for the positive.

Managing your energy and mindset are vitally important in business. As a business leader, others – be they customers, employees or suppliers – will look to you for leadership and guidance. Sinking into a big vat of despair when things get tough does not help anyone. Be mindful of your energy not just for your own sake, but also for the sake of those who look to you and work with you. Bring the optimism and solution seeking positivity and you will be a leader worth following.

Let the right ones in

Surround yourself only with people who will lift you higher.

Oprah Winfrey

If the collective energy of your group is so powerful, it stands to reason that it is important to be mindful of the composition of that group. Having great people surrounding us, influencing what we do and having a really good, deep knowledge base make all of the difference. Look at the people you surround yourself with. Energy is transferable. So what does this really mean? It means who you choose to spend your time with really does make a difference, so pick your tribe wisely.

Energy vampires

You must also always be aware of the impact that the energy of others has on your own energy. Energy vampires are unfortunately all too common in this world. They lurk at every corner, waiting to suck the very lifeblood from you and drain you of every ounce of happiness that you have.

The important thing to remember with such people is this: you cannot change them. The reasons for this could fill another book in itself, but just know that you cannot rescue them from their gloom. Avoid them. If you cannot avoid them, actively manage them to limit your contact with them and take steps to wield the emotional garlic of keeping your own focus on the positive to minimise their impact on your own energetic state.

Bigger future versus bigger past

Let's think of our people as bigger future people or bigger past people. Bigger future people are looking ahead, looking forward to development, looking forward to new opportunities. They desire that next level and want to make the next-level choices. Bigger past people look backwards: they look to past times. For them, the past was bigger and better. They drive looking in their rear-view mirror, and they will do this for the rest of their lives.

Bigger past people may have limiting beliefs, or they may have had a bad experience. Surround yourself with bigger future people. Bigger past people suck the life out of you. They drain your battery, whereas bigger future people charge that battery. They light your future up and inspire you. This doesn't mean you don't need to see bigger past people – you just can't allow them to rob your confidence and energy.

Be very aware of how people influence and affect you energetically. Be very careful of whom you let into your life. Manage entry to your circle. We are not talking about behaving like an egocentric narcissist here: simply be careful of those you surround yourself with as a form of practising self-care. If you are going to do great things, you have to look after yourself.

Be careful of whose advice you take

In addition to knowing who would rob you of every bit of energy you possess, you also have to beware of the advice givers. These people have walked a path and want to tell you all about it. And yes, they may have walked a path, and yes, they may have something to share (after all, it is not cool or a good idea to think that we know it all, because we most certainly don't) – but always apply a critical mind to the information you are offered.

Think about whether you would want to swap lives with the person giving you advice. Often the people who aren't in anyway qualified to give you that advice are the ones freely offering it to you: the single person telling you exactly how to run your relationship, or the regular employee letting you know exactly how your business should be run.

The person offering the advice may have walked *a* path, but they have not walked *your* path. What was right for them might not necessarily be right for you. Or it could be an absolute gem of information. Always apply your brain, practice critical thinking and don't just follow advice blindly.

You are not everyone's cup of tea ... and that is ok

So in all of this, pick your tribe wisely. Be a strong magnet to those you want to attract.

On the flip side, be okay with the fact that you really are not for everyone and everyone is not for you. That really is perfectly normal. Not all clients in all businesses work out. Sometimes, for reasons you cannot control, a client will go elsewhere. Be okay with that.

It is actually better that a client leaves or you don't work together than to have false relationships. Eliminating negative or false relationships and replacing them with positive, true relationships and creating space for inspiring ones is key.

A solid tribe behind you and what you do helps to challenge you to be your best self, the best version of you that there is. There is no need to be too cool to attract your tribe: be you, be real and be authentic to who you are. You will never regret showing too much gratitude, too much kindness, too much joy, too much passion or too much love.

What is a tribe anyway?

Building and growing a community is more about what you put in than what you get out. Don't make friends just to make friends. Build the right community who will give you the strength to really go forward, to act on your ideas and to help inspire you to be the very best version of yourself that you can be.

You may have heard the saying 'your tribe is your vibe', but what exactly is a tribe? Your tribe is your clients, fans, friends – the people who surround you and what you do, and who resonate with your business, training or world view. How you build the tribe of people you want around you and help to grow their positive influence on you is key.

If you take all the individual parts of a piano and set them on the floor, they cannot make music. Put them together, however, and, well, that's a whole different thing. The whole is always more than the sum of its parts. Combining our energy with the energy of others allows us to reach further than we could on our own. Collective energy is a force of nature: leverage the energy of your group to turbocharge your business endeavours.

You can do what I cannot. I can do what you cannot.
Together we can do great things.

Unknown

Finding your tribe

This has always been for me so very crucial, so high on the agenda. It is a lifeline for the tough days (we all have them). The tribe: those people are awesome. They are a key driver for me and they *always* push through, like a beating heartbeat, a pulse, something that thrusts you forward, helping to ensure that your energy keeps pumping, your ideas flow and, well, everything keeps ticking along just as it should, and the momentum and energy in motion simply flow.

So what even is a tribe?

A tribe is a positive social division consisting of families, friends or communities linked in some way, with a common feeling and mutual culture. It's human nature to search for significance and belonging. We naturally gravitate towards those who reflect the kind of qualities we admire and desire. To say we are looking for 'our tribe' means that we are looking for people who share some level of commonalities, similarities or possess the traits we aspire to have ourselves.

Whether it's a training club, a family, community, or group of fellow practitioners, our tribe is important because it reflects our deep and our true values, while simultaneously satisfying our need for companionship.

I've found my team, my tribe, my passion and I live with
passion and laughter now.

Michelle Taylor, Gamechanger

And how do I find one?

That being said, finding a tribe can be tough. Doing so requires effort, authenticity and confidence.

Here are our top ten tips for finding your tribe:

1. Do some self-reflection

Spending time on yourself is always a valuable investment. Developing an understanding of who you are and what you want is always worth it. By developing an awareness of who you are, what drives and inspires you, and what you are looking for, you'll be able to search for relationships that will bring you satisfaction, fulfilment and joy.

2. Try new things

Take that leap. Take a risk and sign up for something new. You'll meet new people and have new experiences. You'll also learn what it is you like and don't like. You'll work out your magnets, and you will then be more able to narrow down the list of things and types of people you want to make space for in your life.

3. Get involved, get connected and put yourself out there whenever and wherever you can, whenever you get a chance

A great way to get started is to look into what meet-ups and clubs are available. There are hundreds of clubs dedicated to various topics and you will find something that excites you makes you feel awesome. It doesn't even have to be about dogs.

Do what makes your heart sing, what makes you happy. When you are happy you will perform better in every single way possible. And the skills you will learn about connecting with others will ultimately benefit you in your dog business.

4. Ditch being judgemental

Remove judgemental tendencies from your world. It is hard: we are very much programmed to criticise, but wake up to being overly critical and make a conscious effort to avoid it. Being judgemental stops us from being able to connect with others properly.

When approaching a group of fellow humans, whether old friends or new, look for what it is you have in common and what you enjoy about them. Find the good stuff; find something you want to connect with. Be kind, always.

5. Know when to commit. . .and when to walk away

Know when to commit: fully, wholeheartedly and as your best self. Trust your gut – your inner feeling. Know when you are on to a good thing. Whatever that is, try to make the effort to keep it an active part of your life and fuel that fire whenever you can.

Conversely, if something makes you feel unhappy, drains you and doesn't light you up, then these are good indicators that it is not for you. Really examine those feelings so you can challenge why you feel that way and consider whether it might be better to walk away.

6. Call out to your tribe

If you know the type of people you want in your life, the types you want to surround yourself with, then make it known. You can use social media to find them. It's likely there are many people who are longing for a similar group, to feel a sense of belonging and a shared identity with a group of close, like-minded friends.

You may be surprised at the amount of feedback you receive when you approach your truth with full authenticity. Your true authentic self is your best self and it's good to release that.

7. Be the first to reach out

When looking for your tribe, you'll be required to kick shyness to the gutter. You need to inspire and attract your tribe. When you meet those lucky individuals who light up your life, channel your inner bravery and ask to connect with them – make your move. People love to hear that they are loved, enjoyed, respected and admired. Connect, connect, connect, and then watch your tribe expand and grow in all the right ways.

Be brave. If it doesn't challenge you, it won't change you.

8. Love yourself

Some days this is tough, but deep down this is truly vital for the bigger picture. Success and feeling great start with you. In loving yourself, you become more confident, more positive and more attractive in every way. It is a growth area for everyone, for sure.

Not only will you feel more comfortable approaching strangers and random people in your world, but you'll also attract exactly the types of people you want in your life. Now how cool is that?

We love being around compassionate, curious and confident people because it takes the pressure off having to please everyone around us. As you begin to increase your tribe, know that you are loved and that anyone who surrounds you is super lucky to know you. You = awesome. You = a unicorn. You = more than enough. Don't ever forget that. Virtual high five to that!

9. Look for and take opportunities

Take opportunities to dance, to have fun, to laugh, to play, to see family, to work with a new connection, to try new food, to dress differently, to let your hair down, to go to a party, to go to the cinema, to travel abroad, to fall asleep under the stars … you name it, say yes, say yes. It is a super cool way to approach life. Our Pro Dog Trainer tribe are grown with this energy and mindset.

10. Take a risk, look ahead, develop a growth mindset

Take a risk at *any* opportunity. Open your eyes to the many growth opportunities in the dog business or any savvy business opportunities that pass you all the time. Always, always ask the question, and never, never be embarrassed, scared or afraid. Always seek out that moment – grow to be the bigger person you've always wanted to be. Live the life you've always dreamed of – live happy, live full, live big. Live the life you love and love the life you live. If you are scared, sometimes that's the perfect opportunity, because that's just the moment you need to dig deep and to well and truly risk moving forward, risk moving ahead.

Enjoy the journey

As I continue to build my own tribe, I've realised that it is a gradual, fun process that develops over time. You culture and nurture it along the way. Life is a journey, not a destination, and we learn on the way. The key is to remember to enjoy the whole ride.

As you continue to grow, you'll learn so much more about yourself and attract more energetic, beautiful, intelligent, mindful souls into your circle. Switch your light on, make sure people are aware you are looking, activate yourself, be brave to reach out, and relish your honest connections that genuinely nourish, brighten and lighten you. Find and love your tribe, and when you find them love them hard.

Standing on the shoulders of giants

Bernard of Chartres compared us to dwarves perched on the shoulders of giants. The metaphor expresses that we can see more and further than our predecessors, not because of our own abilities, but because of the work and achievements of those who have gone before us. From our standpoint atop their shoulders, we can see further and reach new heights of achievement. Give thanks for those that have gone before, then get out your binoculars and toolkit and prepare to make a difference.

But don't just stand there

Sometimes it is worth seeking out and finding professional help for your business. If you feel you need such help, seek it out now, as you know that often later becomes never. Procrastination is not your friend. Make your move, there is someone waiting to help you. A mentor, a coach, a professional could be just the step that you need, and there are many professionals who will be itching to work with you at this level, and will help to laser target and focus that inner passion you have.

With our Pro Dog Trainer tribe we coach our students at this level because we know this is the level that most dog training businesses miss out. People want to make the leap to having their own dog businesses but they overthink, procrastinate, get lost inside their heads, underact and the dream stays just that – a dream. Decide and do. Let others lead small, timid lives, not you. Decision is power.

ACTION TAKER TASK: Make a decision every single day. List the decisions you have made over the last week. Be a true action taker, and make decisions now. What actions can you do at this very moment to take your business idea forward?

DAILY DECISIVE ACTION PLAN

THIS WEEK I DECIDED ON DAY...	ONE ACTION I TOOK TO MAKE IT HAPPEN
1:	1:
2:	2:
3:	3:
4:	4:
5:	5:
6:	6:
7:	7:

Consider a mentor

Know what you want to achieve and consider whether you need help from a mentor to help you attain it. If so, consider what you need from your mentor. Match yourself to a mentor who makes your heart sing, align yourself with a coach, get a technical expert on board, look for the opportunities. No one will hand it to you on a plate. And where would the fun be if they did?

The age of the gatekeeper is over

Don't wait for someone to choose you. The age of the gatekeeper is over. The image of the Willy Wonka Golden Ticket or that 'winning the X-Factor' ticker tape moment is all very attractive, but it is absolutely not required for success in this day and age. We have all the tools we need at our fingertips to create and go straight to our market. Let the market decide whether you deserve success, not a public phone-in.

Enjoy the view, then get working

Your mentor, your coach, your online tribe, your friends and those you admire, those who have been there before and those who have strived valiantly before you – all those are your giants. Watch them closely, and study them gently but diligently. Get passionate about learning and growing in a new way. The vista of possibility lies before you.

Superhero seeks sounding board for mad ideas

In addition to having a mentor, having a buddy or a like-minded, level-headed friend is also very useful. This may be your Pro Dog Trainer tribe friend, a dog training buddy, a business colleague or a growth mindset friend. You don't even need to be close geographically these days – with technology being as it is, your buddy can be located anywhere in the world.

Personally I prefer to work with someone I'm not in any direct competition with so that there is never any conflict of interest or any struggles on either side. I also prefer to work with someone out of my area just for clarity. However, be as flexible as you can so you are both comfortable.

My buddy is someone that understands my business, my ethics and morals, what I do and what I currently don't do, and gets my client base. She is a friend but is also able to put on her critic's hat and critique what I do at a higher level. She is someone I can be truly open and honest without judgement, but she also helps to keep me accountable and gives me a space to bounce ideas.

Having a buddy allows you to work through struggles, tease out logistics and sometimes ditch some ideas altogether. The entrepreneurial life can also be quite a lonely one as not everyone really 'gets' it. Having a buddy with whom you can chat to through the highs and lows can make all the difference to your enjoyment of the journey.

Finding your buddy

Top qualities in a buddy to look for:

- Someone you trust
- Someone you enjoy chatting to
- Someone who understands your business model
- Someone who will be honest with you
- Someone who you are willing to take feedback from
- Someone who you feel you can help in return
- Someone who shows up
- Someone you feel comfortable talking to
- Someone who will help keep you accountable

ACTION TAKER TASK: Find your sidekick. Do you have a buddy already? If so, shout out your sidekick's name here and give thanks for their awesomeness.

FIND YOUR MENTOR / ACCOUNTABILITY BUDDY

	JON	SUE	DAVE	CRAIG	STEVE
TRUST	✔	✔	✔	✔	✔
ENJOY CHATTING		✔	✔		
UNDERSTAND BUSINESS	✔	✔		✔	✔
HONEST		✔	✔		
TAKE FEEDBACK FORM			✔		✔
YOU CAN HELP TOO			✔	✔	
SHOWS UP!	✔		✔		
COMFORTABLE TALK TO			✔		
KEEP YOU ACCOUNTABLE					✔
TOTAL	3	4	7	3	4
			WINNER		

If not, jot down some ideas of those who might be up for the role, or places you might be able to find such a buddy.

Superhero seeks sidekick

While your sounding board buddy helps and supports you emotionally and psychologically through the entrepreneur life, your sidekick is someone who is going to roll up their sleeves and step up to the coalface beside you. Your helper is a critical part of your business: they are the lifeblood, the next generation. They have a vital role to play.

The helper role allows you to delegate and allow someone else some responsibility and gives you the opportunity to outsource the things not meant for you. Giving your helper the chance to take on tasks allows them to grow and develop. As you learned by doing the tasks, they too can learn by doing. It builds confidence and skills in your helper, and also frees up your time to work on other aspects of the business.

Your helper can supercharge your team and can be that voice that allows new questions, new perspectives, new passions and ideas, and new experiments. Think about what, when, where, why you will need your helper, to enhance both them and your business. What can you do to make sure both grow?

Your helper will give you support and allow you the opportunity to grow a team member. This will add to the strong team around you and help to grow your commitment to achieving success and outstanding growth.

Developing a helper allows you to contribute to someone else's learning. You grow by helping them grow, which is pretty awesome. Then at times you will be able to draw on the help of your helper and team member when needed. It is a win-win situation.

The essential sidekick questions

So let's rewind and go back to the who, what, where, when and why.

- Who you're growing is super important: you are going to invest a good deal of time, effort and skill into this relationship. You are going to impart a great deal of knowledge and be very open and real. You've got to have mutual trust.

- What you're growing is crazily important: be aware of what you are cultivating in your helper, what are you growing them to be, how that will fit into your team and how it enhances your helper.

- Where you're asking for their expertise and where you're using them to help you: what skills do they bring to the table straight off the bat, and how can these be utilised? What skills require to be developed? Where can you place your helper in your business so that they can utilise the skills they have now, while growing and developing new skills?

- When you're utilising their skills: you might not need support all the time, so don't try to use all of their time. Grow exactly the model you would like while helping to grow your helper.

- Why you're teaming up with them: you are going to help grow them, grow your business and free up your time to allow space for new projects, experiments and passions.

It's really important that we consider all of these aspects with a potential helper. Find things that are really going to help to develop and improve the whole team as and when it's appropriate and when you feel you need to develop both your helper and your team a little bit more.

Timing is everything – don't throw your helper in at the deep end.

It's also got to be 100% appropriate for the stage that you and your team are at. All too often we see a great, keen helper who has been pushed too far and too fast because we think they can cope. The helper needs to be ready.

As a general rule, we go with the 'watch one, do one, teach one' process. The helper should follow these steps:

1. Watch a dog and handler training session.

2. Do the exercise themselves in a low-pressure situation with a straightforward dog.

3. Teach someone else to do what they have just watched and done.

Using this process takes allows the helper to take the appropriate level of responsibility for the process. It ensures that they are supported at all stages and able to ask questions when they need to. It creates a safe framework for learning. It also ensures that they get a good quality learning experience and that errors are kept to a minimum.

Finding the balance

It's really important that we coach and that we get the balance right between coaching and knowing when to let someone take the ropes. Their progress is not simply down to them; some of it really does come from us knowing when to let them take on a little or a lot. While we want our helpers and team to be passionate and keen and raring to go, all smiley and bright eyed and bushy tailed, at the same time we've got to find that balance. It's important to note what they get from their role, so take a moment to find out what is *their* powerful why.

If things are going too far in the direction of your helper losing confidence, then we need to just adjust and tip back the other way. You need to fine-tune things, because it's completely in your hands and in your power to grow that helper.

It's exactly why we structure the ProDog Trainer Programme as a 10 week online experience – we know we can take you from where you are right now to running a high impact dog training business in that time, equally without overwhelming you. We know because we have seen the hundreds of transformations through the programme with our own eyes.

Make time for your helper

Ensure you make time for coaching and learning with your helper and your team. Communication is key, so make a communication schedule: pop some time in your diary to touch base with your helper and team. Set that date, take action, make it happen. It can be hard to carve out that time when you are busy 'doing' your business, but it is a vitally important investment of your time so don't be tempted to skip out on it.

Even if you can only spare five or ten minutes, do it. It gives the opportunity for sharing feedback, ideas and creativity, and for resolving any issues. It sets focus, ensures everyone is pulling in the same direction and creates drive. It is a bonding experience. You are building your relationship bank account. It will make your helper and team feel like human beings, not human doings. The investment of time will pay dividends in terms of team morale, ability and effort.

It isn't just the learner who is learning

Even when teaching, we learn. Which is great as we always want to be learning.

One model we have had huge success with is 'Train the trainer'.

Train the trainer is when you actually spend some time together – maybe an hour, or a half day – and you train together and train each other. You exchange experiences and learning points, share perspectives, consider things from new angles, and make a mind map together, and come up with new ideas and new experiments to take the business forward. You chat and workshop and create together, and it's an energy-rich opportunity to learn.

You're setting up the potential for a better relationship bank. You're setting up the potential for creating and coming up with new ideas. Training the trainer allows for so many areas for growth on any team.

Building a team

There is no I in team

The more I watch, develop, learn and grow, the more I value the team. For me the team is everything and leading that team through the sunny days as well as the storms is vital. My team started in my business as simply my mum taking the register. I hugely valued her support and most of all her just being there for me. In a whole new world of work, I so needed her there.

I went from one established career and switched to the extreme opposite – a dog trainer, my true passion, and over the years my team has grown from volunteer staff right through to full-time salaried team members, full-time trainers and an office team. There is always room for growth.

Here are just a few of the things we have observed as important:

- All of the team members want and need to feel valued.
- The moments in between the work are important.
- The experience of being in the team is as important as the work.

- The leadership of the team is always at the forefront of our minds.

- We consider all ideas from our team members to be valuable and we appreciate each person individually.

- We are always, always trying to improve communication. Facilitating communication is essential. And it is never done.

- We always try to bring our attention back to the higher goals.

- We encourage sharing within the team of all resources and ideas and suggestions, and, yes, that certainly does include the chocolate biscuits. In fact, it's an obligatory part of being on our team.

- We have a solution-based, growth mindset and I try to delegate problem-solving tasks to the team, because developing a problem-solving, creative, solution-based culture is for sure the way forward.

- We hold regular team meetings to ask questions and offer help. These meetings really help to keep the common goals.

- We encourage idea generation, and we encourage team members take ownership of a task. This works so well both ways, because we empower our team and we free up some of our headspace for new tasks.

Finding great team members

For me personally, finding great team members is possibly the single most difficult task that I tackle. It is super tough to find capable, hard-working, passionate, dedicated and loyal team members, who want to stay and work with you on your team.

In the dog training world, your team members may be (and have traditionally been) involved on a volunteer basis at some level. Some simply volunteer to help out for the purpose of developing their own skills. Never forget that they are still a team member and should be allowed equal credit.

Value your volunteers. As your business grows and your team's ability and productivity grow, you never know when you might look for your volunteers to become staff. A rising tide floats all boats.

I have learned:

- To trust my gut

- To always go with my instincts, because intuition doesn't lie

- That someone who is hungry to learn is worth their weight in gold

- That passion and grit are more important than qualifications

- To give it time: the right team member will come, so never rush

- To be always open to novel ideas

- To be always willing to think outside the box

Picking the best

We're a team and within that team I always fully consider dynamics and energy. Surround yourself with people who push you to do and be better, without drama, judgement or negativity. Just people who seek higher goals and higher motivation. People who seek good times and positive energy and not jealousy or hate. People who know that simply being together brings out the very best in each other. For me, that's the feeling you have in a great team.

Although the right team can make such a huge difference, however, individual team members can be so very variable. Here are just a few simple things to consider when looking for a team member in your dog business:

- Never go solely on qualifications, for surely some of my very best team members have had none, and the most qualified have sometimes been the most precarious, prickly and potentially damaging to my business.

- Run a practical interview, with animals. Never just sit and talk about it – let them show you. You will quickly see what you have in terms of a future team member.

- Offer a trial month for both of you to see how it fits.

- Do things properly: have a contract and ensure you cover all eventualities.

- Try to let your clients know that you are looking for the right team member but don't feel bad if you don't offer the job to someone close. Sometimes, however, the very best team members are friends of friends or friends of close relatives.

- Always take references but never be afraid of someone who hasn't had any dog experience but is passionate and willing to learn. These are some of the very best team members we have had. Passion is everything.

- A team member who is aware of privacy, social etiquette, social media policy and more is also worth their weight in gold. Once again, these little things count more than anything for the business to excel and skyrocket to the top.

- Be willing to grow your own team member. This way they will have the right skills and you will have taught them from day one. It is a pleasure working with a home-grown team.

Qualifications versus experience

I remember some years ago, when I was looking for an apprentice. I interviewed hard. I had someone in mind. I knew exactly what I wanted in a staff team member, or so I thought. I took on two team members that year: they were very, very differently qualified. Let's call them Tiffany and Gemma. Tiffany was very well read. She had a degree in animal-related sciences and behaviour and was doing her master's in animal sciences. Gemma had no qualifications at all. She had left school early but had worked with different animals all of her life.

A few months later, Tiffany was travelling with one of our dogs and a terrible accident happened. To this day, we still don't really know the circumstances exactly, but we received a call from the main road. Our young and sweet Border Collie male, Riot, full of hopes and dreams, crazy full of energy and enthusiasm, had been hit by a car at the side of a dual carriageway where Tiffany had stopped temporarily to adjust the dogs. He died instantly. He was a beautiful dog. He left this world at just four years old.

Gemma was robust, reliable, unable to spell and without any level of qualifications other than those she has acquired with us and obtained from the University of Life (possibly one of the best universities in the world) is still a strong and well-valued member of the team today. She is reliable, honest, dedicated, selfless, smart, hard working and, most importantly, passionately devoted to what she does. For Gemma, we know what she does is not only a way of life – it *is* her life. She is hugely valued on our team, and can turn her hand to everything and anything.

When who we are and what we do become one, we are truly aligned and we love our lives. Our lives are whole, we are fulfilled and work isn't work.

> *Good teams become great ones when the members trust each other enough to surrender the 'me' for the 'we'.*
>
> Phil Jackson

Abundance

It can be quite a scary prospect to reach out to people to talk about your business, to let them in on your ideas and to share your ideas with them for the purposes of taking things forward. But have an abundant attitude to learning and sharing and giving because you actually gain a lot from sharing.

You discover things yourself from sharing with other people. It's highly likely that the more you have an abundant attitude, the more that it will be reciprocated and that people will share right back. You get what you give.

Don't be a hoarder

Sometimes people get anxious worried and guarded about sharing. They get worried in case someone runs away with their idea or in case someone doesn't like it, or maybe they're worried that the energy isn't right. *Interrupt yourself!* Where is your attitude of abundance? Abundance is knowing that everything is going to be fine because you truly believe that there's more than enough for everyone. The more you share, the more you grow.

ACTION TAKER TASK: Develop your interruptor. Have a hairband or an elastic band on your wrist, or even be ready with two fingers to pinch yourself. Every single time you have a negative thought, a non-abundant thought, a judgemental thought, kick in the interruptor, ping that band or pinch yourself. Don't just use a little one – I mean pinch yourself so it makes you take notice and really acts as a deterrent. Just interrupt that pattern of thought so you don't go down that route. You can be better and you are better than that.

Mastering the art of delegation

So now you have your sidekick, a helper and a team. You are on fire. But once you have your team, what do you do with them?

You utilise them, of course.

Let them do things. Trust them to do stuff. Let them take responsibility and handle tasks.

The art of delegation allows you to master your dog business at a higher level.

> *No man will make a great leader who wants to do it all himself or get all the credit for doing it.*
>
> Andrew Carnegie

The D word

Delegation is the assignment of any responsibility, task or authority to another person. For me, it is the subdivision and allocation of many tasks. Often I delegate tasks that don't have to be me, or tasks that are more generic in their outcome, but even this can be a tough decision. For some people, delegation is one of the toughest business skills to master.

For someone who has built your business from the ground up, it is tempting to think that no one can do things like you. But if you have picked your team carefully and trained them well, and if you have identified appropriate tasks to delegate (i.e., ones that do not absolutely have to be done by you), then there is no reason why the tasks cannot be perfectly correctly, capably and confidently carried out by members of your team.

You cannot do everything. You will not be able to sustain the effort and you will burn out. You need to free up some time and mental bandwidth to invest in and create new opportunities to drive the business forward. You've got to be able to work *on* your business, not be stuck working *in* it all the time. And that makes delegation an absolutely essential skill to master.

The benefits of delegation – more than just getting things done

So why is delegation essential in any great business? Delegation can, and when done well will, hugely transform your business. It saves time, increases efficiency, helps build skills, can motivate people and can really help to grow team morale.

Giving 'em all away

So, most importantly, we need to consider which tasks to assign, when, where and how it will all work.

For me personally, I'm a bit of a control freak. I see that this is typical for entrepreneurs and business owners alike so I am certainly not alone. This is not, however, an excuse not to delegate. There are too many benefits in delegation – so get out of your own way on this one. Stop trying to do all the things.

Consider the complete opposite: consider not delegating. Consider that we stay a one-person band forever. For many, not delegating really is a recipe for disaster, or at least a recipe for limiting potential growth or opportunities, and for sure a clear way of 100% guaranteeing staying very, very small. No business can be successful as one person on their own. A team approach is always of benefit.

So at the ground level, what does this actually look like?

First, make a list of all of the tasks that keep your business afloat.

Once you have a completed list, you can then isolate the tasks or a small chunk of tasks that can be tackled by someone else. Handling customer service, maintaining the calendar, dealing with client intake and producing newsletters are perfect tasks for delegation. Ideally there are step-by-step processes that anyone could follow so that these are very easily repeatable. Anyone office based could be trained in these. Delegate these tasks.

Write out instructions for each task and train your assistants to carry them out. Help them, oversee them and expect mistakes. For example, ask to be copied on all emails – that will allow you to make tweaks and adjustments to make sure you are happy with the whole process. Give them feedback. Training someone new can take between two weeks and six months.

Clear deadlines are also key. We need to see the project management working for everyone. Remember that remote virtual assistants are hugely popular, as are distance staff. Remember to always think outside the box.

Going forward into leadership

Are you comfortable with calling yourself a leader? Let's touch on the importance of leadership, as it is vital in your dog business. It is also key to consider it as leadership rather than management: it is about inspiration, trust, growing and developing your team, and giving as much as receiving.

A business needs a great leader. What does it take to be a great leader? What are the characteristics of leaders who are thriving? What do they do differently?

Characteristics of a great leader:

- Has a clear vision

- Has passion

- Has empathy and patience

- Is adaptive and changeable

- Incorporates all knowledge into your process

- Has the ability to listen

- Has emotional intelligence

- Is action oriented

- Is aware of diversity

- Has positive energy, enthusiasm and eagerness

- Responds and is in touch with everyone's needs

- Has a sense of humour and fun

- Has a high standard of excellence

- Has the power or ability to influence

- Has an ability to find solutions

- Is proactive

Anticipate change

Where are you looking to anticipate the next change? Your business model or your life? Look at your calendar – where are you travelling? What are you reading? Who are you spending time with? What's happening in your life? Make a decision right now about some changes so you are prepared and ready to make your move.

Great leaders don't keep their heads down. They have their eyes up and open. They are looking around corners, watching for changes, anticipating what's ahead. Your capacity to look into the future and to plan ahead and anticipate a new move is essential. You need to shape the future and not just react to what happens.

Welcome diversity

What is the diversity measure of your world? Think personally and think professionally. The network of people that you are comfortable with is so important. What is your capacity to develop relationships with people who are very different to you and your capacity to resist the wrong relationships?

Diversity could be cultural, physical, biological, functional, political or socio-economic, and yet, despite all of these differences, people with those backgrounds can connect with you and trust you enough to cooperate with you to achieve a shared goal. Having a more diverse network is going to help hugely in coming up with solutions because you have people surrounding you who think differently from you, and challenge your thinking.

Do not fear change

Are you courageous and brave enough to abandon a practice that has made you successful in the past? Great leaders dare to be different. The most impactful development and change come when you are able to build the emotional stamina to withstand people telling you that your idea is naive or reckless or just plain stupid. The people who will join you are often people that think differently, and therefore are willing to join you in taking a courageous leap.

This will determine your success as a 21st-century leader. These are women and men who are preparing themselves not only for the comfortable and easy predictability based on yesterday and the past, but also for the realities and changes of today and all of the unknown possibilities of tomorrow and of the future.

Be brave

1. Establish and maintain boundaries: you teach others how to treat you, so make boundaries on what is acceptable from the outset. Set out what is ok with you and what is not, and let others know. Humans welcome boundaries as they let us know what is acceptable and what is not and thus removes fear of acting inappropriately from the interaction.

2. Reliability: know who you can rely on, who you can trust and who is welcome in what you are doing.

3. Accountability: hold yourself and others accountable. Put measures in place to indicate progression and completion of a task, and the outcome of same. As is often said, "that which is measured, improves". Be honest and real in your discussions and relationships. Be prepared to give and receive honest feedback – it is the way to grow.

4. Confidence: how do we keep the confidence of others? Looking after each other confidently and with confidentiality is key.

5. Say no to irrelevancies: how do we maintain integrity and not allow ourselves to get involved in rubbish? How do we say, 'You know what? I'm not sure that this conversation is productive'?

Connect

People are wonderful, but they can be hard work. Navigating the demands of our everyday and business lives can be really tough. It can be inexplicably hard, and the people surrounding us can push us to the very edge of our nerves and our comfort zones. The key is always to remember that it is very rarely personal. The person's behaviour says more about them than it does about you. So always seek to understand before you seek to be understood. Don't retreat behind barriers: look for common ground, seek out the connection and always aim for a win-win solution.

CHAPTER 4

THE OWNERS WHO NEVER ACCEPT A RELATIONSHIP AND DOG ARE LOST

Growing great clients

I began to realize how important it was to be an enthusiast in life ... if you are interested in something, no matter what it is, go at it at full speed ahead. Embrace it with both arms, hug it, love it and above all become passionate about it. Lukewarm is no good.

Roald Dahl

You are going to develop your optimistic owners and people surrounding your business. They don't just arrive like that. You are going to grow them. Optimism is something that you can develop in the people around you. It is something you are going to foster and teach at every level and enhance through your journeys together. The solution seeking can be grown and the suffering can be reduced.

So how do we grow great clients?

Connect with them

Work out exactly what it is that your client is looking for. What specific need do they have? Once you know that, you can help them to meet the need, and then challenge them appropriately to get to the next level to take them wherever they want to go.

Be you

Dare to be different. Talk like a real person, be accessible and don't be afraid to show the true you. The world is full of fake. Do remember, however, that a degree of personal and professional distance is still always healthy. Being authentic does not require you to air your dirty laundry.

You don't have to be someone you are not. Just be the real you and amazing things will happen, and amazing people will connect. People love to connect with others. It is human nature. Think: how can you help to make that happen? What can you give your clients?

Respect begets respect, generosity is valued and reciprocated, and being helpful is loved and gets you noticed. Be the voice that people look forward to hearing from. Remember, people buy from people, so be you.

Keep it real

So what does that look like practically? On a day-to-day level, stop with the small talk. I know, that's a tough one. It is so deeply ingrained. Most people would rather talk eternally about the weather than venture into discussing anything personal.

So be bold: ask your clients questions that you want to hear the answer to and that they will want to answer. For example, what was the most exciting thing that happened to you this week? Now, that's an interesting question! I'm at the edge of my seat wanting the answer to that one. A question like that gets your client's brain going, looking for positives, being excited, sharing something with you – that all builds your bond.

Give them confidence

Instil confidence in your clients. Use statements such as:

- Yes you can
- You guys have got this
- You are more than good enough
- I can help you with that
- Let's do it together
- Yes, I understand that, and I can see what you are talking about – let's work through that
- I know exactly what you are talking about – we have been there before
- I'm here for you, just ask

Let your clients know you have their back.

Get them not just to take, but to implement, your advice

Something that we hear so often from trainers, behaviourists, vets, etc., is that compliance is really difficult. Compliance means getting someone to do something that you've suggested to help their dog in some way. So it's in their best interest, and the best interest of their dog, for them to comply with what you're saying, but sometimes that just isn't enough. So how do you make compliance attractive?

Your role is to work out how to make compliance appealing. Threats and warnings of dire consequences if your advice is not followed are not our style and are unlikely to work in any event, so how do we encourage compliance?

Involve your client in developing the solution. Someone is more likely to stick to something that they feel engaged in having developed, rather than having it imposed upon them. Help your client to understand what is in it for them and their dog. Help them to see the benefits of complying with your recommendation.

Listen to any concerns they may have and help them to overcome them. Answer any questions they may have to ensure that they fully understand what to do, and be available if they require any assistance once they have started doing the work themselves. Check in with them. If they are encountering roadblocks to implementing your recommendation, help them to get past them.

This is an area where many dog training businesses fall down. It is not enough to simply tell your clients what to do. Don't just throw the advice out there and leave them to it. You need to work with them every step of the way to ensure that they are able to implement your advice. Cultivate compliance and you will be onto a winner. If you can crack compliance, you will see results. Your client will be thrilled and will return, and will tell others about you. You will be seen as someone who gets results. Your reputation will grow and your business will flourish.

Guarding the energy

Your business venue is a secret weapon in attracting and retaining clients. You know the feeling when you walk into a place and you think this is a really great venue? You can feel the buzz, you are comfortable there, you want to work in the space. It all just feels right.

That is the energy you are seeking to create in your business venue. Make it a place your clients want to be, and the business element almost becomes secondary. Your clients will actively seek to come to you, with no selling or persuasion needed, because they just enjoy being there.

Taking care of the basics

Fancy new premises might just not be an option when you are starting out, but the key is to make the best of what you've got. Make sure it is safe for dogs and their owners so that both can relax. Make sure the temperature is comfortable and it is well lit. Make sure both human and dog needs are appropriately taken care of to ensure comfort. Go for decoration that suits what you do: bright colours for fun and energy, and pastel or light colours where calm is needed.

What we don't want

We all know of spaces that drain every bit of energy. I previously experienced one such training venue. I walked into a space set up for dogs and their owners. Every part of this space lacked energy, and every part actively sucked energy. On arrival, the office door was stiff. The place was cold, and no one looked up from their desk as I walked in. In a place like that, the staff turn up late and leave early, and when you call the staff on the 'team', they really don't want to speak to you. Everything really is too much trouble. You will all, I'm sure, have experienced something like this, and this is for sure not the energy space you want to create.

The secret sauce

Even if you don't have money for a fabulous bespoke venue, taking care of the basics will give you a good, solid, energetic basis for your work area. Then you add the secret sauce: you. You bring the vitality to the venue. Make it your space, set the enthusiastic tone, and make it somewhere that people and dogs just want to be. You are going to do that even before they have set foot through the door.

Begin to set the energy level from the outset through your correspondence with your potential clients and existing clients, whether that is through emails, social media, phone calls, text messages, direct mail, etc. If you're not feeling great, don't answer the phone. I know that sounds crazy but let the call go to voicemail and return it as soon as you feel you can.

The lunch-time phone call example

A Monday lunch at East Bowerland Farm is a busy hive of activity, with the holiday cottages and all the dogs and all the people. It is a fun time, it's a great time and it's great together time for everyone on site. Some days lunch is fresh garden produce; other days it is wholesome soup and freshly baked bread, or maybe it's fresh root vegetables and quiche. It is a busy affair, the builders, the office team and whoever is home wants to be there, and the more we grow the bigger the lunch affair becomes, yet it's a tradition we enjoy.

On one particular Monday, just as the hustle and bustle settled and we sat down, the phone rang. No one responded, because everyone was looking forward to lunch. My mum finally got up and answered it, but with a tone of irritation. She wasn't irked by the client; she was annoyed by the situation, but in that moment the client felt her frustration. The moral of the story is, set some boundaries and guidelines. We now delegate the phone so we know exactly who should be answering it at any one time, and this applies to all similar scenarios.

Never answer an email right away, unless you are certain of the answer. Give it ten minutes for you to figure it out and to get it straight in your head. Switch the phone off or have an out-of-office message if it is not appropriate for any reason to delegate answering to someone. Always remember to manage your stress bucket. Your client's first experience of your business, or their 100th experience, is so valuable. Set that energetic tone from the outset.

Visualisation

Set your energetic intention from the outset by visualising how your class or client appointment is going to go. See yourself being calm, but energised, with everything running well and you handling everything beautifully. Be positive and let the Universe know that you are open to and grateful for everything going well.

Manage the energy on arrival

Sometimes the minute your students, clients or potential clients walk through the door, they will jump on you before you have had a split second to summon the energy or implemented any strategy to take care of it. That's something that you need to plan for. Be ready for them. Have their workstations set out and ready to begin working at. Have some quick tasks ready and get them straight on task when they arrive. Change the energy before they change it for you. Energy is something that is really hugely manageable, adjustable, flexible and transferable – never forget that.

Guarding your own optimism

So how about you? How is your energy? How is your optimism? Sometimes your task might actually be to work on yourself as an instructor. Working on you is always a good investment. People can sense energy, and energy draws more energy.

People can utilise and draw from your energy. That's effectively what dog trainers, instructors and behaviourists need to be astutely aware of, because often people come to you in a very low energy place. The struggles that they experience or the reason they got a dog in the first place isn't matching up to their reality and what's in front of them. Their energy is depleted because they're struggling with that situation, so you have to bring your energy and share it. Your energy becomes the fuel for their successful dog training results.

That makes your energy bank crucially important. You have to look after your own energy reserves and keep them topped up. Self-care is vital. Know what raises your energy and what depletes it. Rest, recover, make sure to restore your energy between classes and appointments.

Topping up your energy bank

Just as we know about the relationship bank account in dogs, we all have an energy bank. Our energy bank account gets replenished and depleted by the everyday occurrences of life.

Here are some things that we find top up our energy banks:

- Candles

- Scents

- Music

- Training our own dogs

- Walking on the beach

- Family time

- Hold a glass of water to the sun and let the sun's energy infuse the water

The list is absolutely and completely non-exhaustive. You will know what pays into your own energy bank and what takes from it. If you are unsure, simply take a moment to pause and really consider how something makes you feel. Be very aware of your body's response: do your shoulders slump, do you frown, do you smile, do you stand straighter? Your body will tell you the impact, and it will also let you know where the balance of your energy account currently lies. If you are feeling chipper and ready to go, then your account is in credit. If you are feeling low or sluggish, then energy funds are low and you need a positive energy top up.

So how do you make this relevant and completely work for you? Life does not just hand you positive things to put into that energy account we talk about. Or so you would think. Sometimes it is just a case of opening your eyes to what's already there. I was chatting to my team on this only the other day, about how magical it is that at just the right time, at every corner our business turns, we seem to meet just the right person to push us to the next stage. It is an incredible feeling. Always remain open to the positives and they will appear.

ACTION TAKER TASK: What tops up your energy bank?

RE-ENERGIZE BANK...ENERGY TOP UP

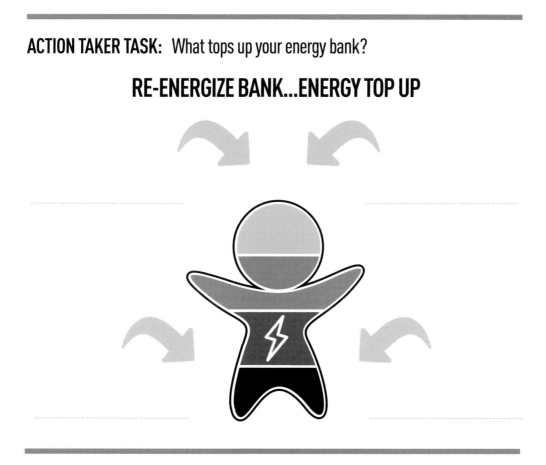

Fake it 'til you make it

Sometimes you may have to fake it 'til you make it. Sometimes when you've got a class, you may be feeling a little bit low on energy, but bounce around, clap your hands, get excited, do whatever helps you to fake it until you feel it. It could be music, or it could be adding in a certain smell. Or just try starting with a big smile, whether you feel like smiling or not. Whatever it takes.

Have some tricks up your sleeve for raising your own energy. Know what brings your energy up and gets you ready to rock and roll. It could be having a shower, going for a brisk walk, listening to some '90s dance tunes, a particular food – anything that gets your blood moving and gets you ready to go.

> *The absoluteDogs team is helping me learn how to develop my own concepts, especially my optimism, confidence and tolerance of frustration. They've taught me the importance of the energy I bring to every moment – don't just turn up, show up. A happy trainer gets better results.*
>
> Zoe Swan, Gamechanger

Spreading the energy

Creating optimistic clients

Sometimes you need to change the mood around you, especially if you are teaching in the dog business world. Your clients are going to come in and you've got to remember that your owners may have had a bad day. And they will bring that with them. Be prepared because this will happen.

Be ready to manage the energy from the moment of meeting. Take control of the energy of the meeting and be ready to bring it up or down as is necessary.

The communication between you and the owner in terms of feedback is absolutely crucial to creating an optimist and developing an abundant mindset. Leading by example means that you're going to pick 'what do I want' in many of your day-to-day situations.

Let's say you see a 'what don't I want' – I don't want you to pull your dog around on the lead like they're some kind of puppet.

What you are going to say is 'What I'd like you to do is really effective and super achievable. All we need to do is encourage your pup to follow you and the big challenge is – can you keep that leash loose at all times? Now, that's tough, but I know you are super owners so you really don't need to pull them on leash. Ok — three, two, one, *go!*'

All of a sudden that little reframing is the source of optimism and joy. The framing of the task is the source of energy that is going to propel people forward on their training journeys and excite them.

Keep the wow moments coming

Rehearsal is so important. Your clients come in and they rehearse wow moments. They rehearse uplifted and enhanced energy; they rehearse optimism; they rehearse feeling great, feeling awesome. We've actually reframed the whole class, group, waiting room or groom room, and we're practising what do we want and setting our owners and clients up for success.

Recognise progress

The final point that is absolutely crucial in developing optimistic owners is to recognise the steps of progress as moments of success. Progress really is success in lots of little small steps. Find ways to recognise progress, whether that is letting the group know where somebody is in their development, maybe having a wow moment privately with the owner to say 'that was awesome', or sometimes sending an email or a text letting them know how great something was. Remind them of last week's success and see how you're going to build that progress for this week, or set them homework so they can make some more progress at home.

I always remember one client I complimented after a particularly good manoeuvre. She had an extremely reactive and difficult terrier, and was really not feeling very good about her ability to manage this dog that she loved so much. When I praised her, her face broke into a wide smile, her shoulders straightened and she went on to achieve great things during the rest of that course. To this day, I know that she regards particular manoeuvre as her 'superpower', and it is her go-to tool for managing situations. It's amazing how one moment witnessed and one compliment given can make such a difference.

We often underestimate how difficult it is, when you live with a dog day in day out, to see progress (whether you're an optimist or a pessimist) because you're seeing that dog all the time. You've got to be that person who can radiate that successful positive energy ethos so that people's training or dog ownership journey will be way more fun.

It's going to be something that is recognisable: you can see the enjoyment and fulfilment and everybody is going to feel better, and then be better – the fellow owners and everybody else surrounding what you do and what you share. The key is that everybody is progressing. It just might be that you've got to identify what that small piece of progress is and point it out to them.

Rates of progress

On that note, your classes and your clients will all for sure have different rates of progress. Some students in a class may feel inhibited or anxious about some-body else in the class. One of your roles – and it's a key role as an instructor – is to make sure that everybody's journey is individual and everyone's individual successes are recognised.

Boundaries: the bedrock for optimism

When you run your own business, there will be tough days and maintaining the balance and boundaries can be challenging. When you are faced with so many competing demands on your time and attention, it is essential that you have the self-awareness and self-discipline to set effective boundaries, both for yourself and for others. Knowing what is absolutely 'for you' or must be done by you and knowing what is not is crucial so you can avoid the time sinks that can easily suck up your time.

Remember that you are running a business, not indulging in an expensive hobby. Both in terms of time and financially, know your numbers and do the maths. Work out what your time costs. Then, if someone asks you to do something, gives you a job or offers an opportunity, take time to evaluate it against these calculations. How does it stack up? Is it worth it?

Bear in mind both the financial cost of an opportunity in terms of materials (such as room hire for consultation, business insurance or travel costs) and in terms of your time (how much time will you have to use to complete the task). Also factor in opportunity cost – if you do this task or take this opportunity, it means that you will have to say no to other opportunities. This is life, and deciding by definition means to cut off options. However, it pays to be aware of what you are sacrificing in order to take a particular opportunity, because it keeps you firmly focused on making sure that the opportunity is as right for you as it possibly can be.

Saying no is not just ok – it is essential

You will be presented with many opportunities and ways to fill your time when running your own business. Do not be afraid to say no. Rehearse it if saying no is something you struggle with. It is a crucial superpower, so you will need to get comfortable with it.

Saying no does not mean you are unhelpful. It does not mean that you are not a solution seeking optimist. It means that you are a grounded, sensible business owner who recognises that there are only 24 hours in a day, that your energy is precious, and that you are able to manage and allocate your energy reserves appropriately. Now *that* is a superpower.

Boundaries rock

Like dogs, humans work extremely well with boundaries. We are social creatures who live in family groups – we expect boundaries and rely on them so we know how to behave. Utilise this knowledge to create a framework that lets your clients know what is acceptable in their relationship with you.

For example:

- Have a set office or work space

- Have a work phone number and email

- Establish some level of boundary for friends/clients

- Fix set work hours where possible (although it's great to be available, it can come at a price so it is key to find the balance)

- Be disciplined in taking time off – try to separate yourself from your business and give yourself clear down time

- Don't answer correspondence 24/7

- Manage your screen and online time

CHAPTER 5

TO THE GAME PLAYERS

Concepts

Concepts in dog training is something we are hugely passionate about. We train our dogs using games and concepts. We are the fun makers. Here are some of the key concepts we work on in our dogs:

- Grit

- Independence

- Optimism and confidence

- Self-control

- Arousal concepts

- Focus

- Flexibility

- Proximity

Concepts: not just for dog training

But what about training ourselves? Well, these concepts can play a huge role for us too and are the perfect concepts to develop in ourselves as action takers in the dog business world.

So what do these concepts mean to us as action takers?

Grit: problem solving, resilience, tolerance of frustration, the ability to get up each morning and keep going even when things are tough.

Independence: of mind and spirit, the ability to think and make decisions for oneself – this is the bedrock of leadership.

Optimism and confidence: the ability to look at a problem and think 'I can solve that' and the self-confidence to take that solution out into the world, tell people about it, and charge appropriately for your time, energy and resources in developing and making it available.

Self-control: the ability to delay gratification, to make good choices, to recognise and value yourself and what you are trying to achieve, and to not let the clamour of life distract you from your mission.

Arousal concepts: thinking despite arousal, calmness – being able to keep a clear head and remain calm is crucial in business. Arousal up/arousal down is also massive – the ability to manage your own energy is key to ensuring that you don't burn out.

Focus: the concept of champions. In a world that lauds multitasking and constantly split attention, being able to laser in on what needs to be done will set you apart from the masses. The very act of focusing and taking something forward is sadly something that many will never be able to do. The lure of multiple channels of such easily accessed distraction available in the modern world is unfortunately the graveyard of many business dreams. But focus matched with action is unbeatable.

Flexibility: always keep an open mind. Focusing on your goal is a must, but always be prepared to be flexible in how you get there. Rigid thinking sinks business ships. Never be so closed that you can't consider an option. Having been examined, it can always be discarded. Iteration, pivoting, learning are all fruits of open, flexible thinking and key to growth in any business.

Proximity: just as proximity work teaches your dog that you are the centre of all that is fun in the world and being near you is *the* place to be, so it is for your clients. Be awesome. Be fun to be around. Make interacting with you a pleasure. Bring something real and valuable to the lives of your clients.

Rock those concepts

So here's to the game players, the most innovative and exciting and successful people in business – and that's any business not just dog businesses. Gamechangers will have many of the above qualities by nature and will be working on many others from the list above.

The list is by no means exhaustive. We could add many more concepts to it – Gamechangers are always seeking to grow, after all. These are just some of the core concepts that are commonly seen to build success in the modern world. I simply love that what we want to grow in our dogs is exactly what we want to grow in ourselves. Now that is magic.

ACTION TAKER TASK:

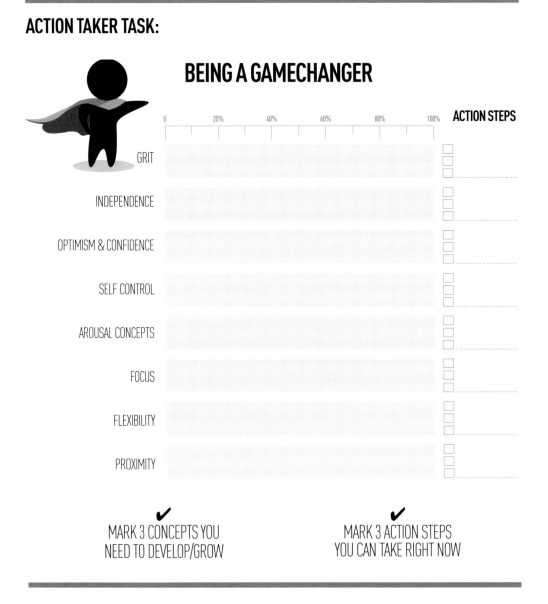

BEING A GAMECHANGER

	0	20%	40%	60%	80%	100%	ACTION STEPS
GRIT							☐ ☐ ☐
INDEPENDENCE							☐ ☐ ☐
OPTIMISM & CONFIDENCE							☐ ☐ ☐
SELF CONTROL							☐ ☐ ☐
AROUSAL CONCEPTS							☐ ☐ ☐
FOCUS							☐ ☐ ☐
FLEXIBILITY							☐ ☐ ☐
PROXIMITY							☐ ☐ ☐

✔
MARK 3 CONCEPTS YOU
NEED TO DEVELOP/GROW

✔
MARK 3 ACTION STEPS
YOU CAN TAKE RIGHT NOW

No one ever wants to do public speaking

Public speaking is something generally feared and avoided by most adults. It is up there on the high stressors list with moving house and getting divorced. But as a business person, you will need to be able to speak publicly about your business to represent it out there in the world, so public speaking is a necessary skill.

We will all deal, at some level every day, with the public. So public speaking is always going to be a good skill to add in business. We could all develop this skill for the better, to boost our confidence and to keep us growing on every level.

Confident public speaking is just another rehearsed skill. It is something that you can learn, something that you can practise, something that you really can move from your conscious to unconscious state, something you grow into, and something that gets easier with effort and preparation. It will also boost your confidence once you get over the initial fear (and fear isn't a bad thing either – it just shows that you care).

Remember, expecting things to change without putting in any effort is like waiting for the kettle to boil without switching it on. Change starts with emotion and then taking action, as hard as that can be. If public speaking is not your thing, embrace the change. Start small – chat to strangers as you go about your daily business, then build up. It doesn't have to be a big, formal, business speech. Just look for opportunities in your day to talk about your business to strangers.

The public speaking nightmare

I remember the day very well when I spoke publicly for the first time. I was 20 years old. I stood up in a classroom and tried to explain to 32 15-year-old students one of Shakespeare's key lines. I was nervous – well, petrified actually. I kept my eyes down, and I couldn't stop shaking. I froze. I couldn't read. When I tried to write on the board, my hand wouldn't stop trembling.

I felt awkward, embarrassed, and very, very small, but not so small I was invisible. I felt shame: shame for my inadequacies and shame for the failure I had just endured, painfully I might add (they were 15 year olds after all, not the most forgiving crowd).

The reflective practitioner would always ask: what could I do to ensure it doesn't happen again? What could I do better?

Here is why I didn't perform well that day. Can you relate to any of this?

1. I was not remotely prepared, and I had never had any level of feedback. Practise, practise, practise! It is so simple, and yet so often overlooked. Practise to your dog, whether it's asking for money from a client, feeling comfortable explaining what you do or teaching a group. All of these take rehearsal unless you are that one person in a hundred who feels naturally at ease in these situations.

2. I did not truly believe in what I was sharing. You can only share messages that you can truly relate to, you live, you practise, you believe deep down. Then you can articulate it. Make sure if you are selling and sharing ideas, they genuinely connect with you and genuinely matter to you. Today I know I'm a Gamechanger, and it's in my bones. I truly believe it, to my core. It is easy for me to teach others these concepts when the belief runs through my veins.

3. I was worried about what people thought about me. We get so fixated on how we look that we are obsessed by what other people think about the whole experience. That paradigm needs to be switched. We are there to serve the people we are communicating with. But it is not about you: it is about the audience, the students, the clients, your new customer and their canine companion, the people surrounding you. Think about them. This is their experience. And this applies to absolutely everything. It really is all about them.

So after all of this I dusted myself off, I got back up and I tried again. After all, a winner is just a loser who tried just one more time.

So how did I get better at public speaking?

I practised. I took any opportunity and I spoke at vets, at schools and to various audiences, of all ages. I spoke to my dogs. I rehearsed in front of a mirror. You name it, I did it.

I tried to ground myself before ever starting anything. For me that meant physically grounding myself, touching something with my hand so I could anchored myself; I would leave any bad thoughts there. It is vital for me to settle my nerves and cope with them. Enabling in your mind the calmness that it needs will facilitate great confident and authoritative public speaking.

The most useful of skills

You never quite know when public speaking will come in handy. Be authentic, be real. It is exactly the reason you will be truly heard. I remember being in a very important planning committee meeting, possibly one of the most important days of my career, my business, my home – my life – and I was feeling physically sick. I stood up to address the planning committee, about 30 appointed councillors who sit once a month on matters that the local council cannot resolve.

I cleared my throat, my paper shook, and I looked up. The panel felt very cold. I could feel their judgement and they hadn't even spoken to me. I took a long deep breath and I addressed the committee: "I'm really nervous. In fact, I'm petrified. I have never done anything like this before and this means so very much to me. It is so close to my heart. It's my home and my heart and everything I have ever dreamed of, and it means so very much. I want you to know that, so I'm going to give it a shot, because this really matters."

And with that I immediately felt at ease. The councillors warmed to me. That day not only was I liberated from my fear of public speaking but I was also set completely free of eight years of planning struggles, neighbour wars and ongoing battles. For my parents and our family, it was a huge day of celebration. As we came out of the meeting with all of the quarrels having been set straight and the council having voted unanimously to support our small, home-grown, passionate, Devon-based family business that employed many local services. This day was and still is a huge one in our lives, and one I will never forget – and also one I never, ever expected. I was so glad I could pull out the public speaking card to end what had been a long struggle.

At the end of it all, as we deconstructed the meeting, I spoke to our planning adviser who told me just how much of a difference my speaking personally had meant on this occasion. He felt that it swung the decision completely in our favour with a cold council, purely because of well-researched planning and factual planning law supported with passion, authenticity and raw emotion. I really did feel on top of the world that day, with gratitude over-flowing in bucket loads. Never, ever, give up. I'm still smiling this writing right now.

> *Be yourself; everyone else is already taken.*
>
> Unknown

Top tips on public speaking and confidence building

- I filmed myself (easy to do on almost any mobile by propping it up, or you can even treat yourself to a selfie stick). I rewatched, critiqued and tried again, and it got better.

- I asked others to observe me. I wanted to see how others perceived what I was doing. I started with people I felt comfortable with and then gradually asked people who would maybe critique me harder.

- I practised, and I practised a lot, and then I practised some more, some-times in front of a mirror, sometimes alone, sometimes driving in a car (please stay focused on the roads). When I felt I was ready, I practised for real, in front of smaller audiences. Practise until you can deliver the information in a natural way, without having to read slides or notes if possible. No one wants to watch you read your presentation.

- Get smart, get knowledgeable, do your homework, study your topic. I became obsessed with learning. I still am. You can learn so much from so many varied places. The opportunities are endless.

- Engage with your audience, whether that's one customer or one hundred. Engagement and connection are so very key. Find any topic that allows you to connect, on any level, and when you do, embrace it.

- Pay attention to your body language and work to change it if required. Be aware of the signals you are sending out with your body position and movement.

- Prepare, prepare, prepare to the max before the event – do your home-work on every single part of the assignment, from finding out about your audience, through preparing your subject, making sure you are well groomed and have planned what to wear, to doing a dry run to the venue so you know how to get there and how long it will take. And once you are there, practise in the actual place where you will deliver your presentation. Get a feel for the acoustics. If you are going to be using a microphone, practise using one.

- Think positively. Think great things and use affirmations to help grow you. Affirmations are positive powerful statements that can help you to challenge and overcome negative thoughts. When you repeat them often enough and say them out loud, you become them and believe in them, and they become meaningful to you. They are a positive mental exercise, allowing positive patterns to be formed in your brain and enabling us to think and act differently.

- Be ready. Prepare a very short introduction of a sentence or two, to keep in your toolbox for those moments when you have the opportunity to discuss your business. Your introduction should explain who you are and what your business does.

ACTION TAKER TASK: Create your own affirmation poster

Examples:

I am enough

I have the power to create change

I am an excellent public speaker

YOUR AFFIRMATION POSTER

ACTION TAKER TASK: Write your intro and test it to make sure it makes sense and conveys the necessary information to someone who doesn't know your business, then practise, practise, practise. Practise it until you truly do not need to think about it. Then, when the moment comes, it will just roll off your tongue.

YOUR INTRO...IN A NUTSHELL

I AM A INSERT YOUR SKILL HERE   WHO INSERT WHO YOU DO YOU HELP/WHAT YOU DO/PROBLEM YOU SOLVE

BY HOW YOU DO IT

SO THAT RESULT YOU ACHIEVE FOR THE PEOPLE YOU HELP

EXAMPLE

I AM A DOG TRAINER   WHO HELPS DOG OWNERS WITH REACTIVE DOGS

BY CREATING WORKSHOPS FULL OF CLEVERLY DESIGNED GAMES

SO THAT THEY CAN HELP THEIR PET BECOME CONFIDENT AND RELAXED WITH THE WORLD AROUND THEM

The skill of skills

For me, confident public speaking leads to so many other areas in developing any dog business, or any business at all. Confident conversations, socialising and networking between like-minded souls is vital to the success of your business.

Before speaking publicly, or before I get into any important situations, I always consider my state. So what do I mean by state, and is it changeable?

Your energetic state

Your energetic arousal level, or state, is something with which our Pro Dog Trainers are very familiar. We actively seek to ascertain and manage our dog's state or arousal level, but how many of us practise it on ourselves? Being aware of your own energetic state is key to peak performance.

Knowing how and when to relax is obviously a great thing, but for our Gamechangers and ProDog Trainers, knowing how to turn up the energy and bring your A+ game is equally important.

So how do you bring the energy up? Here are a few of our top tips for raising energy levels:

- Jump around (think House of Pain's song 'Jump Around').

- Play engaging music, music that buzzes, music that gets your energy up.

- Eat a high-energy snack, drink water, look after your body.

- Listen to an energising podcast.

- Find someone that inspires you and energises you in person or online and spend five minutes charging.

- Join the ProDog Trainer Tribe.

- Motion is generally powerful: go for a brisk walk, go for a run, add motion to your day.

ACTION TAKER TASK: How do you change your state? List five ways to bring your energy up and five ways to take it down

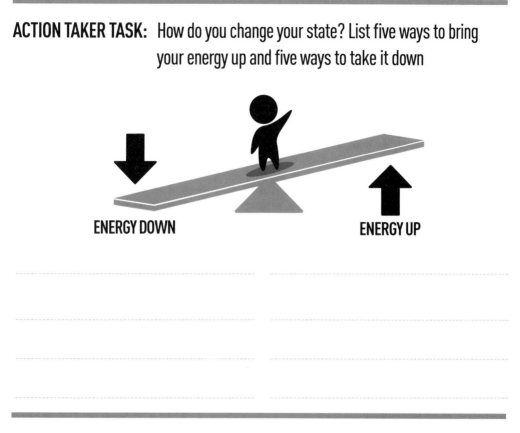

ENERGY DOWN   ENERGY UP

When to change state

When do I change my state, and more importantly when should you change yours? A change of state is often a good move. Maybe you want to speak publicly, you want to make a big decision, go into an important meeting, ask an important question, do a demo in public – you name it, any occasion that matters may require a change of state. Get practising, and jump around. Emotion is energy in motion, and changing emotion is what stands out and what makes a difference every single time.

Your own personal development is key for growth. This is for you as an individual, you as a student, you as a trainer – it is on all levels. Always be looking and moving in the right direction, taking every opportunity to leap or creep forward, staying on track, staying positive. It is hugely motivating and it will leave you feeling energised.

Progress and taking steps forward is one of my favourite motivators. It's in my very core. And every time you flex this muscle it gets easier. Every time you practise it requires less energy. Training yourself is so important in running your own business. Know growth areas, know the motivators you have and stay accountable to your why. For me, progress really and truly matters, at every level.

The mind gym

Another of my favourite ways to turbo charge my energy is spending some time in my mind gym.

What is a mind gym, I hear you ask.

The mind and body are intrinsically linked, and sometimes the incessant chatter of the mind can tire the body. The mind gym is where the mind is calmed and realigned with the body through physical exercise.

Entering the mind gym allows me to get into my peak zone and stay there longer. It enables me to focus, create and find wicked solutions for wicked problems. It gives me a vibrant certainty in what I do and helps hugely with project "change my mental state". It maximises my productivity and energy, and supercharges my sense of purpose.

Creating your own mind gym

Look for any sort of physical activity that helps you to re-frame or shift focus, i.e., makes you put your everyday thoughts to one side for a while and concentrate on the physical activity you are doing. My favourite examples are:

- Yoga
- Beach walks
- Walking my dogs
- Swimming
- Ice baths
- Running

Entering the mind gym allows you to reconnect body and brain. It realigns your systems and gets everything firing together. Find your favourite mind gym activity and go there as often as you need to keep mind and body working in harmony.

And if it all gets a bit much...

The demands of daily life are many and varied and even the brightest, solution seeking Gamechangers can have a bad day. If it all gets a bit overwhelming, try this mini version of the mind gym: take a deep breath. Taking a deep breath reconnects body and mind by focusing the mind on the act of taking the breath (the physical). It gets you out of the thoughts that are troubling you and fuels your body with the oxygen it needs to go forward. Let the air filling your lungs calm and recharge you. As you breathe out, let go of any worry, and send peaceful and loving thoughts to all.

The joy of designing your own day

We really have the privilege each and every day to design our day and not feel bad or guilty about it. In running a dog business, you will truly get to design your day. It's about balance, it's about your energy and your awareness of your energy. It's about how and what you communicate at every level.

Looking after yourself and designing your day are crucial. You will also be able to design your day around the types of clients you have, or other factors – perhaps you have an elderly dog, a child, a dependent family. Whatever it is you design your day around, it's something that you really have the ability to truly shape and action.

When you master the art of designing your own day, it doesn't have to be the normal. Get creative. You can go crazy and design what works for you. Often when you're really passionate about something it can become all consuming and become an absolute monster. Deliberately designing your day is absolutely crucial to get the right message across, to get the right energy across and to stop your business from becoming your jailer.

Make sure you are prioritising things that are going to make you feel great, whether those are family, friends or whatever. Then shape your world and your business around those priorities. And that means in your diary, whether it's a day planner, a week planner, a month planner or a year – write those things in pen that you should not compromise on. And stick to them.

ACTION TAKER TASK: Design your perfect day

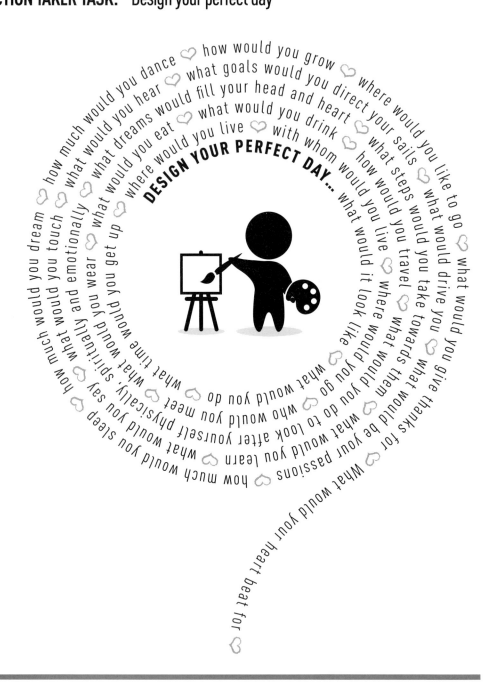

DESIGN YOUR PERFECT DAY... how would you grow ♡ where would you like to go ♡ what goals would you direct your sails ♡ what would drive you ♡ what dreams would fill your head and heart ♡ what steps would you take towards them ♡ what would you eat ♡ what would you drink ♡ how would you travel ♡ where would you live ♡ with whom would you live ♡ what would it look like ♡ what would you do ♡ who would you meet ♡ what would you learn ♡ how much would you sleep ♡ what would your heart beat for ♡ What would be your passions ♡ how much would you look after yourself physically, spiritually and emotionally ♡ what would you wear ♡ what time would you get up ♡ how much would you dream ♡ how much would you touch ♡ what would you hear ♡ how much would you dance

Practical tips for making your day your own

Here are a few top tips that have helped me design my own day.

- Limit access to technology – we all know that our technology can become so consuming that sometimes we're not even aware we're completely absorbed by it. Sometimes technology can go to the point where you're not even present in the real world. So don't allow that mobile phone, that piece of technology, that email, that text message, that work injection to take over. Design your day – it's really important that you keep hold of your day. My latest strategy (as it's an ongoing challenge) is to monitor my screen and social media time; I try to reduce my screen time and up my creative time. It is an ongoing battle but I'm winning, and I set you the same challenge.

ACTION TAKER TASK: Manage your screen time and social media time. Actively record the amount of time screen and online time you spend in your day and then try to reduce it. There are apps available that can record your phone use. This task will massively open your eyes to your time use, and may very well help you identify some time that could be freed up either for your business or relaxing, as required.

- Life's not fair – control the controllable. Don't focus on the things you can't control, so let go of those and focus on what you can do. When a game plan doesn't go to plan, change the game plan – and know when to move on.

- Play your own game and don't spend time focusing on others.

- Dare to be different.

- Have a year planner and be fixed in your outcome but flexible in your approach.

- Map in all of your most important diary events first: holidays, family time, birthdays and occasions that matter to you. Then map in your work time after that. This doesn't mean we can't be flexible, but having the big, important dates in place first means we don't have to try to squeeze them in later when the diary is filled.

Opportunity knocks

Opportunities are usually disguised as hard work, so most people don't recognise them.

Ann Landers

Looking for the right opportunities is key. At different times in your business you may want to expand what you are doing, or narrow it and work with a niche. This really is all open to the individual needs of any business at any one time.

Risk going forward, seize the day and don't wait for luck. Be an opportunity seeker and actively seek out the right opportunities for you.

You will never be spending time badly when you invest in you, the game player. Personal growth, development and progress are at your very core. Motivational and growth opportunities have a huge impact. By focusing your thoughts on learning, growing and uplifting ideas, your subconscious will begin to implement a positive pattern in your way of thinking and your whole outlook on life. Your positive energy will attract opportunities to you – get out there and grab them.

CHAPTER 6
THE FUN MAKERS

Dare to be different

There is no passion to be found playing small – in settling for
a life that is less than the one you are capable of living.

Nelson Mandela

You are wonderful, you are special, you are unique – whatever and whoever you are. Being okay with being in the minority or being different is a part of being who we are, standing out, standing up, knowing deep down that we are never, ever alone. We are all in this together. There is a different way to live in this world, so stand up and say 'I'm ready for it. This is me.'

Take time to be fully present, show courage, show shame, have moments of spiritual awakening, be grateful for the gifts of imperfection, and take the opportunity to practice gratitude at each and every opportunity. It is awesome to be different.

The most pervasive disease is the disease of being normal. Who has achieved an extraordinary life by being bland, by being normal? Welcome weirdness. No one 'normal' ever dared to be genius, willing to risk uncertainty and vulnerability, to really create a change. Shift perspective and express who you are. Be different. Embrace weird.

Different will make you stand out. Different will catch your customers' attention and providing something different from the norm will make your customers want to join your tribe. And adding fun to the mix just takes it all to the next level.

While I was scrolling through Facebook, I came across Tom and Lauren from absoluteDogs. I noticed they were a bit different from the others I had seen before. They showed me another way, fun and clever games-based training that I could fit into my busy lifestyle. With a full-time stressful job in London, this was exactly what we needed. As I started to see changes in Pixel through the games, I suddenly became passionate about the possibility of helping others who have similar struggles. I wanted to tell the whole world there's a game for that!

Cathy Tse, Gamechanger

This is me

You make the choice: are you going to show up and let yourself be seen?

Let go of the fake, the pretence. Be around authentic people. Be yourself – authenticity is a practice and a way of life.

Let go of perfection, because it really does not make you happy. It is an impossible standard that will rob you of happiness. It will keep you striving for a world that doesn't exist, and prevent you from enjoying the one that does.

You have come here so that you may become. Become what, you may ask? The primary question is 'who should I be'. So many of us ask this same question of ourselves. You are here because you are restless. Deep down, you know you are more, you know you have more and you know you have more to give to the world. I know that I can help you seize the life you always wanted and that you deserve. Forgive my passion, but you are more than good enough. No matter what society says, we – that's you and me – know better. So ditch normal, and get out there and be you.

Sometimes you hear something and you are simply ready for it. I'm in, I'm ready. Are you ready?

Happiness is when what you think, what you say, and what you do are in harmony.

Mahatma Gandhi

The joy of vulnerability

So what does it mean to dare greatly, to show the courage to be truly vulnerable, to ask for exactly what you want and what you need, to show up and be fully seen, to talk about exactly how you are feeling, to have the tough conversations? Are you ready?

Most people see vulnerability as a weakness, but I see it as a human strength. We need to live in the space of our own vulnerability and embrace it fully and see it as the true cornerstone of confidence, because unless you can allow yourself the risk, to live openly, you are missing out on so many opportunities each and every day.

As a wholehearted person, you recognise that in reality you are so much like everyone else, which gives you the confidence to be yourself – which is all you really need in life. There is no true intimacy where there is no true vulnerability.

Step into the light

There is a real freedom in expressing your truth and establishing your boundaries. Such clarity frees you to stay grounded in your values and beliefs, regardless of what others think of you. There is no place for the dark shadow of shame when everything you are is expressed, open for all to see and fully embraced by you. Now that is a position of strength.

We are all afraid. It is in our make-up. We ask ourselves the questions, am I enough? Am I secure? Am I liked enough, loved enough, smart enough? These questions are completely normal. We need to believe in ourselves, hold our own truth, and well and truly let go of what other people think.

> *Be fearless in pursuit of what sets your soul on fire.*
>
> Jennifer Lee

Let go of the need for certainty

It is important that we let go of the need for certainty – it is no good for us. Certainty is born of predictability and predictability is certainly not what we entrepreneurs are looking for in life.

Being vulnerable, not knowing exactly what's coming, and enduring risk and a certain level of emotional exposure are all part of the entrepreneur experience. People love to know, and certainty is secure and prized, but I challenge you to a dare: let go of the need for certainty and be comfortable with whatever happens.

Fuel the fire

Being a fun maker is going to bring you success. The passion, desire, creativity and fire within are key in being an action taker and successful in whatever dog business you are working in. Put logs and sticks on that fire to keep it burning brightly, and don't back off. Whether that means investing in your own learning or connecting and mixing with others with that energy, fuelling the fire is key to maintenance and growth of the soul.

Fun will give you a competitive edge

Being a fun maker also means staying well ahead of the game, in every single way. Whatever it takes, stay both truly committed and focused on the prize. Remember that having fun will naturally take you to making progress and experiencing business breakthroughs. Those who have fun and play together stay together, and enjoying the ride is a huge part of this special journey. Those who are grinding the wheels every day lack the zest for life that lets fun makers grasp that glimpse of an opportunity or embrace that change or give that last push on the extra mile. The ability to have fun gives you an energetic edge. You will shine brighter than your competitors and people will want to work with you.

Take time to reflect and refocus

It's easy to get carried away with life, but always take time to reflect and refocus. A gratitude journal helps. I write things I am thankful for in the moment and something that I'm looking forward to for tomorrow. It's a place to write about what I'm excited about waking up to tomorrow. In writing that down, I set my day up the night before. I project energy and optimism, and I get excited about the invisible world. Invisible projections are very powerful, real and very exciting.

Take those few moments to reflect on what has happened, give thanks for it, check in with what you need to happen next and focus your energy on bringing that to fruition.

Redefining success

> *Everything that can be countees not necessarily count, and everything that counts can not necessarily be counted.*
>
> William Bruce Cameron

Our schooling, parents, the books we read and our world shape our definition.

Most of us identify success as an event, a box, a destination – a thing. But if we redefine it, if we rewrite it, we can actually consider how it could be measured, and make it more tangible and real. It's not about gratification; it's about gratitude. It's not about the size of your home; it's about the size of your heart.

Be mindful

Calming the mind and working on ourselves, chatting with the mind and having healthy conversations, working with our mind to be our best friend, and being able to have a good healthy conversation and dialogue with the mind are all important. You can get into a much better space and you can interact each day with really what matters. Be selective with your diet, whether that's your internal dialogue or whether that's you picking up the newspaper or reading a book or journal, listening to the news or watching a television programme. Be mindful of your diet.

And, in the age we live today, we need to be keenly aware of the complete addictions of social media. We are addicted to the buzz, always wanting something fresh. Social media is insanely time consuming and – suddenly – it has complete control of your day and no longer do you have the power to design your day. It is key to consciously choose and direct your thoughts. Yes, there is for sure space for subconscious brilliance, but we focus on conscious, intentional work that we direct for 75% of the day.

Don't forget the gratitude

> *Trade your expectation for appreciation and your whole world will change.*
>
> Tony Robbins

Don't forget the gratitude

Here's a little story about a diary. I called my hairdresser to book an appointment and asked her to look at dates for me for early in the new year. She replied: "I don't have my January black book just yet! I will purchase the dreaded black book and get you some dates."

I love my hairdresser and she is a great hairdresser, but I'm sad for her. Really, I am. My work, my business, my team excites me. My goal is, and has always been, to create a life that makes me want to jump out of bed in the morning, to have a colourful life, a life I don't need to take a holiday from. I live that life and I want to share that life with you. Designing your day is exactly this on every level.

ACTION TAKER TASK: Today I am grateful for ...

ADD ONE MORE EVERYDAY...

CHAPTER 7

THE JOY FINDERS

When I was 5 years old, my mother always told me that happiness was the true key to life. When I went to school they asked me what I wanted to be when I grew up. I wrote down 'happy.' They told me I didn't understand the assignment, and I told them they didn't understand life.

John Lennon

Love your life

Ignoring your passion is slow suicide, never ignore what your heart pumps for. Mould your career around your lifestyle, not your lifestyle around your career.

Renu Paswan

Some people in life know exactly what they want. One day I woke up obsessed and passionately in love – I'm not quite sure at what age, but I wasn't very old at all – with dogs and all animals. I completely knew from then on. It's in my blood, it's in my veins, it's who I am and it's my passion. And passion is everything. It took me a long time to admit it though, because society didn't deem dog businesses as 'successful'. So it took me a while to gather my thoughts and appreciate the passion and the desire.

By 21, I trusted my gut, found my inner courage. I felt the inner flame. It became my driving force, my powerful why. It shone brighter and brighter the more focus I gave it, the more air time I allowed it. I found my through line, the choice that was right for me.

If I had to give just one piece of advice, just one what would it be?

Live the life you love, and love the life you live. Do what makes you happy, love what you do, get passionate, get real, be your authentic self, enjoy the small things, breathe and breathe deeper, be grateful, enjoy the journey, and celebrate, recognise the people around you, find your inner courage, be brave (it will take you to amazing places), shift to a world of contribution and trusting your heart, your passion, your inner fire, your deep belief, be vulnerable.

It's a privilege to do what one loves, but it's your privilege and your opportunity, and here it is. Virtual high five!

From dream to reality

Don't be afraid to dream big and take a risk. If I hadn't I wouldn't be sitting here this evening thinking about going for a walk with my dogs, planning puppy classes and deciding how I want to organise my very own classroom. You never know where your dreams will take you.

Janine Vander Yacht, Gamechanger

So how do we bring that into our life on a daily basis, hourly basis, or even a minute-by-minute basis? Is it even possible? For sure, the answer is clear and it's a 'hell yeah' (with a virtual high five to boot).

This is what we are here for. This is what we are meant to do. This is our higher purpose, our deeper meaning. It is meant to be, and it's exactly what we are on this earth for: to live, love and experience life. So yes, that was maybe a fraction more than one piece of advice…but we should always be a bit extra, a bit exceptional, just a little bit more. We were not created to be ordinary. Go the extra mile, and risk going ahead to trust in the journey. Be brilliant.

Where do we start?

So how do we turn our dreams into reality? Where on earth do we start? Well, those ideas, those daydreams, those brainstorms, those creative moments, those things you think *really* matter, the interests, the sparks, those deep thoughts, those curiosities, those things that wake us up or stop us from going to sleep, the ideas you are scared to vocalise, the things that stop you in your tracks – those are all are the things that you need to pay attention to. Daydreaming is where your attention goes when it doesn't have the yoke of daily life to shackle it – follow it and see where it leads.

I know these daydream paths so very, very well. I sat in my lecture theatre at law school daydreaming most of the time, rarely present with the law, but far more frequently with dogs jumping hoops – especially those conveyancing lectures, which were the worst of all lectures. Escaping to my creative world was needed.

Take the steps

So those ideas, they are the ones deep in your soul. Take a risk on those, and explore the opportunities that flow from them. You won't always be able to see the next stepping stone. It is not always logical or obvious, and it is certainly unlikely to be laid out for you. And if it is, it is even your path?

Your passion will uncover endless opportunities. Follow your intuition, go with your heart and trust in the Universe. Give yourself time and space for finding the way. The modern world hurries and harries us to know, to decide, to move, to be, to do, to succeed, to go, go, *go*, right now! It is worth investing a little time at the outset to check with your inner compass which direction you should be taking.

From this, establishing yourself and your ideas will grow and you will move from action inertia, to risking going forward and taking action, making quicker and better decisions.

ACTION TAKER TASK: List some inner thoughts, some ideas – don't be shy! Dig deep, be real

MY INNER THOUGHTS, DREAMS & IDEAS
DOODLE SPACE

ACTION TAKER TASK: And now take action!

DAILY DECISIVE ACTION PLAN

THIS WEEK I DECIDED ON DAY...	ONE ACTION I TOOK TO MAKE IT HAPPEN
1:	1:
2:	2:
3:	3:
4:	4:
5:	5:
6:	6:
7:	7:

Find your freedom

Remember we have one life. Just because you have an offer doesn't mean you have to take it. Only you know the landscape of your soul. Just because you have a solid, reliable job doesn't mean you have to stay in it. Just because you are good at something doesn't mean you have to remain on that single path, and just because someone else wants you to do or not do something doesn't mean you can't do it your own way.

Just because a path is mapped out clearly ahead of you, with lights along the way and signposts, doesn't mean it's your path. You are only free when you realise you belong in no place but every place. That is the true beginning, and that is true freedom.

Pay attention to your calling

Here is the thing: only you know the true landscape for you. It is so important to trust what pulls you. Pay attention to the pull of your magnets. People all have their own opinions, but that doesn't make those opinions right. What is right for others is not always right for you. Learn to listen to and trust what feels right to you.

Don't fear the place of not knowing

The place of not knowing and indecision can feel a little scary at times. We are so conditioned to have a plan and know where we are headed and always to try to get there as quickly as possibly that sometimes it can feel like the whole world is charging ahead to some great destination while you are stuck just trying to pull your own thoughts together. But that is ok. It is more than ok. That time and consideration are essential to making sure that the life you choose to live is your own, and not crafted from the expectations or desires of others.

The place of not knowing and indecision is also a place of great potential. It is full of hope, fertile beyond belief, full of promise. It is a sure path is waiting to be created that leads to an extraordinary life, wherever you are right now, from whatever stage you are at. Enjoy the excitement of the uncertain period. You will emerge and it is beautiful beyond belief. Stop asking for the plan and start looking for your passion.

Don't be afraid to return

Once you move on from the place of not knowing and indecision, don't be afraid to revisit it once in a while. As a business leader, there is tremendous responsibility on you to come up with all the answers. If you feel like your inner compass is off, or if things just don't feel like they are going the way they are supposed to, check back in to that starting place. Look for your passion. It may have changed. Listen closely to your heart and you will know how to go forward, refreshed and recharged.

ACTION TAKER TASK: Get quiet and listen to your heart. What do you dream of, hope for, desire, long for? What great things do you see and foresee?

WHAT IS YOUR HEART SAYING?
DOODLE SPACE

A real life example

Everything, every person, church sermon, friend and finally even family alike was saying "Jump! Go for it!" I saw butterflies everywhere. They just seemed to appear ... I was getting the message loud and clear. My time had come to fly. And then I literally flew over to Devon to meet Tom & Lauren in person and do some serious learning.

So, I have been 'flying' since 1 June 2018, and designing my day. I did not realise I was really flying until August rolled around and I realised that, as I sipped my morning coffee and went for a second cup, my teacher colleagues were back at work. All of a sudden, I realised that I was totally responsible for my day and that there was a new puppy that day waiting to begin training and games. There was no one telling me what to do or when to do it. I could walk Jasper whenever ... I now love being my own boss.

Annie Lewis, Gamechanger

The more you follow your hopes, dreams and passion, then the easier it becomes to risk going forward.

Meet Michelle Taylor, a Gamechanger who took that leap...

"When I graduated from University, I ended up working in the oil and gas industry (as many people do where I live) it wasn't really where my heart was but it seemed to fit. But deep down, there was always something missing from my life, a calling – I just didn't know quite what was missing until recently.

For the last few years I've volunteered for absoluteDogs – spending evenings and weekends hearing from people and their dogs, answering questions, problem solving, editing and polishing videos or helping the team out with anything and everything!

absolute-dogs.com
117

Having volunteered for a little while, Lauren first approached me about a job around 2 years ago, and my response was "maybe one day". I said this out of huge fear of change, the unknown I suppose?!

Recently Matt re-presented the opportunity, I thought about it for all of one second, I said "YES!" Why? What changed? Ultimately me! I'm a very different person to who I was back then ... life has changed dramatically, it's different now.

Whilst it's hard for me to write, with tears in my eyes, my tissues beside me and a lump in my throat I think it's important you understand the defining moment that really has changed me, shaped life for me differently and pushed me to take a risk.

A little less than five years ago my Mum was diagnosed with cancer, and two years ago I held her hand as she took her last breath, just two months short of her 50th birthday.

I don't want to dwell on how hard those years were, as it goes without saying, but you need to understand that my Mum is my driving force.

I now realise just how short life can be, and how quickly things can change in the blink of an eye. I don't want to be that person that always says "one day" I truly want to make it "day one".

My mum was brave throughout her illness – she was strong, coura-geous, amazing and had a wicked sense of humour, a really naughty laugh, and it remained despite all she was going through! I want to be that person, the person she taught me to be.

Since volunteering for the team, I can't begin to describe the change in energy between my oil job and absoluteDogs. It's like some sort of drug, I am truly addicted to the buzz and I want more and more. The team, and the people who follow us, are honestly the best people I have ever met and had the pleasure to be surrounded by. We have the best shared energy, and it's fun. For any of you who have been to an absoluteDogs event, or are part of the Facebook groups, you will understand just how amazing it is to be part of this very special community. The power of that energy – it's like nothing I've ever expe-rienced before.

I've also come to realise just how many lives have been transformed through what absouteDogs has to offer. This is hugely motivating and inspiring for me – I want to be part of that journey helping to transform people's lives and helping to guide others when they are maybe struggling.

Working for absoluteDogs will allow me to work from home, I am about to embark on a whole new journey where I can design my day. This means I can dedicate more time to my husband, more time to my dogs and what I want from life, and living it!

It's been a very emotional journey for me and I've had to dig deep to get to where I am now – I'm a lighter, happier and more resourceful and resilient person and am so very grateful to my mum for everything she was and everything she stood for and to everyone at absoluteDogs who have helped me become who I am today. I've found my team, my tribe, my passion and I live with passion and laughter now.

Before Mum died, she spoke at length with Lauren and she told her that all she wanted in it all was for me to be okay, she wanted to know in her last months that I was going to manage and to have friends and to get through all of this and be okay … and now I can finally say that I am. Live with Passion."

Make it happen

So how do you take the invisible and intangible and make it into something you can see and touch? How do you take exactly what you are dreaming of and make it happen, whether it's business, your body, money, life, love, family?

The trick is to make a start. Just take that first step. Whether it is a tiny step or a giant leap, just move.

Make a mind map, write it, vocalise it, share it – these are all simply ways to begin and will help us to make progress. The power of the mind and focus is a great thing and it's amazing what simply writing that down and channelling thoughts towards it can do.

A word on planning

Never wait for the perfect moment, or the perfect plan, or the perfect opportunity. Perfection is a false promise that will keep you stuck in one place forever. You can analyse, plan and think and these will all feel very good and as though you are doing something. But at the end of the day only action will carry you forward. Good enough is good enough to get you moving, and motion beats perfect any day.

> *The hardest obstacle was finding a space to train, with many spaces not allowing dogs, or pulling out at the last minute. Being resourceful, I knew I just had to find a space anywhere to get started. I have found that people are grateful for what you can give them and the venue is just a space to train and any space is better than no space!*
>
> Sarah Jane McLaren, Gamechanger

Ditch 'too busy'

Banish the words 'too busy' from your vocabulary. You are not too busy. Everyone has 24 hours in a day. Really get real about this. Where can you find more time and adjust your day to spend your time better? Do you watch any television? Spend any time on social media? Spend time on your phone? It is not a question of time; it is a question of priority. If you truly desire something, you will find a way to make it happen.

How to find time to make it happen

- Get up earlier

- Go to bed half an hour later

- Use your lunch break

- Don't watch television

- Stay off social media

- Stay off your phone

- Say no to things and don't attend things you don't want to attend – use the time to work on your business

- Delegate – only do things that absolutely require you to do them and cannot be done by someone else

Give a little bit extra to make your dream come true

There is one more thing I want you to think about. If you were to put in 5% more effort, would it make a difference? How about if you gave 10% more effort, would it make a difference? What about if you were to give 20% more effort, would you make a difference?

ACTION TAKER TASK: What more can you do? Where can you find time to work on your dream?

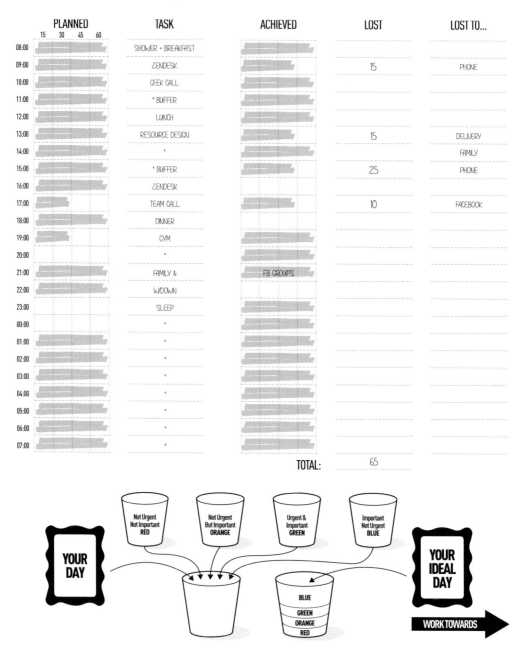

	PLANNED	TASK	ACHIEVED	LOST	LOST TO...
	15 30 45 60				
08:00		SHOWER + BREAKFAST			
09:00		ZENDESK		15	PHONE
10:00		GEEK CALL			
11:00		* BUFFER			
12:00		LUNCH			
13:00		RESOURCE DESIGN		15	DELIVERY
14:00		"			FAMILY
15:00		* BUFFER		25	PHONE
16:00		ZENDESK			
17:00		TEAM CALL		10	FACEBOOK
18:00		DINNER			
19:00		GYM			
20:00		"			
21:00		FAMILY &	FB GROUPS		
22:00		W/DOWN			
23:00		SLEEP			
00:00		"			
01:00		"			
02:00		"			
03:00		"			
04:00		"			
05:00		"			
06:00		"			
07:00		"			
			TOTAL:	65	

PLANNED 15 30 45 60	TASK	ACHIEVED	LOST	LOST TO...
08:00				
09:00				
10:00				
11:00				
12:00				
13:00				
14:00				
15:00				
16:00				
17:00				
18:00				
19:00				
20:00				
21:00				
22:00				
23:00				
00:00				
01:00				
02:00				
03:00				
04:00				
05:00				
06:00				
07:00				

TOTAL: ....

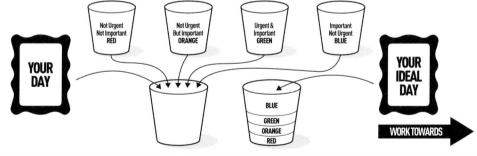

First step, be accountable. Second step, make it work. Third step, just hold on and enjoy the ride.

Becky Beacock, Gamechanger

CHAPTER 8

THE OWNERS WHO INSPIRE RATHER THAN FORCE OR DEPRIVE

Feeling the burn: avoiding professional burnout

What is burnout? Burnout is a state of physical, mental and emotional exhaustion, caused by repetitive and continual long-term demanding situations. Anyone – yes, anyone – can become exhausted and often disillusionment ensues, which can lead to burnout.

Common symptoms are:

- Feeling low energy
- Having a negative or critical attitude
- Trouble sleeping
- Dreading work
- Being easily irritated
- Blaming others
- Feeling empty
- Avoiding daily life
- Feeling your work goes unnoticed
- Experiencing physical complaints
- Pulling away emotionally

How to avoid burnout

This is huge when running your own business, and can literally make the difference between making or breaking it.

1. Work with purpose. Look at the deeper and more meaningful impact of what you do on a daily basis. Think about all of those dog owners who you

help, and how, by helping their dogs, you not only improve their lives but also the lives of all of those around them.

2. Delegate what doesn't need to be done by you directly where possible. If your time is limited, see what can be done to delegate. Don't say 'oh, but I can't possibly delegate' – remember we are solution-based thinkers.

3. Schedule a meeting with your team. If you are the team, then schedule a meeting with yourself. It is important and you need to plan in some time to map out exactly what is needed to ensure that all tasks run efficiently without losing you or anybody else in the team. Making sure you are kind to yourself and your team is vital. If you can't be kind to yourself, your business will suffer.

4. Take a break, regularly. I regularly schedule in break time, including family time, holiday time and recharge-for-24-hours time. I do them all. For me, the beach, the waves, the woods and the trees are full of energy. I try to take myself somewhere where I know there is energy. I recharge the batteries and I come home ready to face the business, the team, my friends and my family with the energy I have gained.

5. Exercise is one of the very best ways to stay motivated, to stay connected with your body, to look after your brain and your mind, and to recharge. As crazy as it might sound when you are feeling tired, get up, exercise, go for a walk, go for a run, get some fresh air and try again.

6. Eat a high-energy snack or drink some water. Make sure you are adequately nourished and hydrated to face the challenges of the day. Always be mindful of your body's energy needs and take care of it accordingly.

7. Schedule weekly good self-care rituals, for example time out to take a bath, read a book, listen to a great motivating podcast, go for a long walk, have a massage or do something that feels just that little bit indulgent. Do it – make time for you. Looking after yourself will keep everything in motion just as you need it. Motion, emotions and action are all intrinsically linked and you need to keep them all in flow.

8. Recharge regularly throughout the day. If you aren't getting up, then get a glass of water – move. Add motion. Motion charges your battery. Change your state, play some music, call a friend, dance, do whatever it takes to stay in that happy, optimistic state of your best self.

9. Change your state. Yes, yes, yes, I know we have talked about this, but really and truly do this at any opportunity and whenever necessary, or even just for the fun of it. It is key for top-level business mastery for maximum productivity in your whole business. Things that we like to do: eat something zingy, jump, drink apple and ginger, dance, use motion to change emotion, laughter (real belly laughter), play music, exercise or go for a run, have scent around us or even on us, and take a cold shower or a hot bath. With any of these you really can change your state.

10. Celebrate good times and achievements. Come on, let's celebrate. Reward yourself. Find things to be happy about, high five, dance, be merry. Remember, it's the little things, because in the end they become the big things. Share the good, and minimise and guard against the bad. Always acknowledge and celebrate your achievements. As entrepreneurs, we are always looking towards the next thing to be done or achieved, and although this is natural, take a minute to appreciate, celebrate and give thanks for the awesome things that you've done already.

Put preventive measures in place and implement these simple practices for allowing and enabling you to be your very best self. For me it's all about the happiness project, kindness starts to oneself, and understanding that is at the very root of a successful business.

Confident leadership

Running a business sounds so cool, right? Powerful? It means leadership, and it kind of says 'I'm important', right? Wrong. Never, ever let your ego get the better of you.

You will attract attention as a leader. People will ask you for guidance, direction, opinion and endorsement. But don't let it go to your head. Stay grounded, stay real, and be authentic and true to yourself.

I have caught myself a number of times going down this path. Be honest with yourself. Stay humble and level headed. Touch base with your values and your powerful why every day, and pinch yourself and self-interrupt if you are losing touch with them, because whether you are losing yourself to your ego in one direction or flagging and worrying struggling with self-confidence, motivation and credibility in the other, both seriously sabotage your ultimate success, happiness and well-being.

Saboteurs

Be aware of your saboteurs. A saboteur deliberately damages or destroys something. In business, you are never going to please everyone. Haters gonna hate, right? But unfortunately sabotage can sometimes come from a place a little closer: your own mind.

Examples of saboteurs

- Being a stickler

- Being a victim

- Being hyper rational

- Being a pleaser

- Being hyper vigilant

- Being a hyper achiever

- Being restless

- Being a controller

- Judging (yourself, others, circumstances)

- Being an avoider

Why on earth would I want to sabotage myself?

There is no rhyme or reason to the saboteur. They pop up at the most inconvenient moments and in the most inconvenient ways. They are simply your brain's way of trying to keep you safe by keeping you within the known. Saboteurs represent your brain's automatic mental habits of limiting beliefs and general assumptions of how to overcome the challenges life puts in front of you. Your brain means well. It is a system that worked very well in stopping us getting eaten by sabre-toothed tigers, but it can be a bit inconvenient in the modern world, causing stress, unhappiness, frustration and other negative emotions. These can be crippling to getting anything done and stop you moving forward.

How to defeat those demons

Never let those demons get the better of you – they are not your path, and they are not your way. They might seem like fearsome beasts but saboteurs are ways of thinking that you have the power to change. Awareness is key to overcoming our saboteurs. Be mindful. Recognise when you are thinking or behaving in a way that might not serve your goals and values. Saboteurs stem from fear so look for clues such as feeling afraid, obsessive, controlling, judging, worried, avoidant, and so on.

Interrupt those thought patterns. Activate a different voice and a part of your brain that has more optimistic feelings such as curiosity, innovation, empathy and creativity. You can change the pattern of thought and change the path to one of positive and affirmative action.

Confidence in decision making

Fail to prepare, prepare to fail.

Anonymous

Running your own business is fun, vibrant, thrilling and, at times, very stressful. Making decisions, staying accountable, staying excited but not overwhelmed – it all takes will power. It takes grit and you have to stay in the game. The life changes can be huge.

Confident decision making is vital. It will enable and facilitate everything you ever wished for.

How to make good, confident decisions

1. Do your homework, research, gather as much information as possible and for sure collect facts, not hearsay. That allows you to assess your options from a place of informed power.

2. Brainstorm and come up with several possible choices and determine if those options are actually completely or at least acceptably at ease and in line with your values, as you will always want to stay in line with and true to your values, your interests and, ultimately, your capabilities and team abilities. Remember to ask yourself 'now what needs to be done?' It has served me very well over the years in running multiple dog businesses.

3. Never underestimate the power of a good, old-fashioned pros and cons list. One sheet of paper, two columns, one for all the positives of a path and one for the negatives. It is a great tool to get all possibilities into tangible, visible form. It helps to organise your thoughts and can be a useful indicator of whether one side obviously outweighs the other at a basic level. I still revert back to pros and cons lists, even if just in my head. I find them such a simple and yet effective way to decision make some days.

4. Ask people you trust on the issue in question or those confidentially in the know. Some will have had similar experiences or have gone though similar processes, and there may be some aspects that you haven't even considered or thought about.

5. Make the decision and monitor your results. Sometimes it's a learning curve, and I love the saying that 'you are either winning or learning' – so it's a win-win.

6. After it all, go with your gut, and stay true to yourself, always. In life, love, business and so much more, I have learned to trust my gut. It gives me the right vibes and always guides me in the right direction.

Remember that no matter how carefully and confidently you make a decision, there are never any guarantees. You will never know in advance whether a decision will work out. Make the best decision you can, and step boldly on.

Don't drive looking in the rear-view mirror

Resist indulging in the seductive lure of looking back with the benefit of hindsight. Hindsight may be a wonderful thing, but what is past is out of your control and looking back is only for learning from history. Look forward. Always, always look for opportunities: if you make a mistake, it's only another opportunity for growth and learning. There is always a bright side. Decisions are often reversible and we can learn every time.

Taking the rough with the smooth

In business you will have tough days, you will have rough days, and you will have up and down, wobbly days. You will have days when you really wonder what on earth it's all about. And then you will have the days when you know that you have truly achieved so much, when it feels so great and when the world seems to have everything all in the right place, and all of the boxes are ticked.

Some days you win, some days you learn. But always, always be kind, to yourself and to others. It's hard some days to find the kindness and the joy, especially when things don't go your way, but find peace in knowing first this normal and second that some things are out of your control. That's hard, but it is as it is. And it is always best to let go of the uncontrollable.

Always aim to make things better

When things get tough, here are a few extra things we do to make things better:

1. Pick the things you are grateful for and focus on the positive.

2. Put steps in place to ensure success, such as some delegation or switching your phone to aeroplane mode.

3. Take a holiday, or at least take a break from it all. Rest up and recharge for ultimate success and productivity.

4. Continue to surround yourself with only awesomeness. Be super picky about who you spend your time with in work, life and play.

5. Accept with the fact that some days are down days and that's ok. Make tomorrow awesome, and interrupt any negative patterns of thought. Don't allow them to creep in. It's normal to have ups and downs – it is life and it is business. The challenge is to not allow it to affect you and to never allow yourself to get into any place but positive.

We are the dreamers of dreams.

Arthur O'Shaughnessy

CHAPTER 9

TO THOSE WHO WHEN FACED WITH A STRUGGLE SCREAM 'THERE'S A GAME FOR THAT'

Sometimes, the struggle is real

Some days it is hard to take action, despite having a dream, despite having a powerful why, despite having an amazing growth mindset.

But the inner soul of a Gamechanger, the deeper soul of a solution seeker, will always overcome all struggles, and overcome struggles in a way that plays to the very spirit of us – by always, always finding a game for that.

Purposeful Action Planning

Our favourite game to get things going from a business perspective is Purposeful Action Planning. You get to have some fun, get creative and really focus on what you want out of life. This is your one shot at this life, so make it count.

Purposeful Action Planning is a step-by-step process that will take you from the bird's-eye view of what you want to do with your life, right through to the daily steps you need to take to achieve it. It is my absolute favourite tool for designing the life I want to live. So get your thinking caps on and jump right in.

ACTION TAKER TASK: Purposeful Action Planning preparation – you will need many sheets of blank paper, pens of many colours, any other art/creative items that you think might assist you in creating the masterpiece that is your life. Find somewhere inspiring to work, have some tasty snacks on hand to keep your energy up and get creating.

The Purposeful Action Planning process

Values

Here is where we find out whether you have been doing your homework. Bring your list of values from the values task in Chapter 1 to the Purposeful Action Planning party. Your values are the things that are important to you in life and so form the foundation for your Purposeful Action Planning work.

Have your list of values front and centre. They are the stars of the show here. Review them. Are they still true and relevant to you? Do they resonate to your core?

Don't be afraid to revise – if anything no longer feels true to you, change it. If you have new or additional values to add, pop them in. Your values list should be a living, breathing thing that reflects where you are and forms a touchstone against which you will measure your decisions, so regularly view it and keep it aligned with your true self.

Vision board

This is where the glue gun and glitter come out. Grab a sheet of paper and a stack of images that form a visual representation of the things you want to achieve in your life. Be guided by your values and really go to town.

Fill your vision board with everything you really want to achieve or have in this life. If you can't find an image, draw one. The more you that you can bring to your vision board, the better.

Bucket list

So now you have a note of what really matters to you and an idea of what that looks like. Your next job is to create a bucket list. As ever, get creative on this. If someone had a magic wand and could give you anything and everything you ever hoped of, if you could have any experience or realise any dream that you had ever wished for, what would it be? Put all those things in the bucket.

This is no place for overwhelm or realism – the beauty of this is that you have your whole life to achieve these things. They don't have to be done tomorrow and you don't have to have all the answers on how to achieve them right now. Just put them down on record so that they are captured and made visible.

Roles and responsibilities

Has ever a task had such a dull name?! We might as well call this section the 'daily grind' and be done with it. Never! We are optimistic action takers and we embrace what we are, who we are and what we do, whether on a daily basis or on a whole-of-life basis.

In this task, you are going to note down all of things you are responsible for and all of the roles that you have. It is key to get these down on paper. All too often we get frazzled by trying to keep track of all of these things in our heads and it all becomes too much. So if you are a spouse, parent, sibling, friend, dog owner, volunteer, anything – note it, then pop a note under it of what the role entails, what your responsibilities are in that role and what you would like to achieve in that role.

This is a really great time to consider what you have on your plate. Really get gritty here, get real on it. What is on there and are you entirely happy with it? This is your life, remember. If there is something on that plate that, if you had the choice again, you wouldn't put on there, consider whether you might want to make some changes. There are always ways to change things up: you can stop doing things, delegate the responsibility to someone else, pay someone to do work for you, politely withdraw from participation, have a frank conversation and change what your role entails … the possibilities for change are endless, so never be stuck. Just because you gave something a place on your plate at one point does not mean it has to be there forever.

And if there is something that you really burn to do, a role you really desire to have, that isn't already on there? You guessed it – get it on there. Now is the time to make sure that this list reflects the you that you are right now and would like to be going forward.

Completing this task sends out a very strong message to the world and to the Universe that this who you want to be. You will find that circumstances and situations begin to align and opportunities will begin to present themselves to fulfil the roles and responsibilities you have declared to be yours and that you want to be yours. Magic.

General get-to-do list

We all have those tasks in life that don't really have a spot within a particular role or responsibility – they are just things we have to do. Get all of the things you have to do out of your head and onto a sheet of paper. You will feel much better for it. Gather them all there and rest assured in the knowledge that they are noted and you will get to them.

The big plans

Looking at your values, vision, bucket list, role and responsibilities, and get-to-do list, what do you want to achieve over the next ten years? Dream big and note it down.

Work back from that starting point and begin to break it down. If you want to achieve this item in ten years, what steps will you have to take to implement it? Where will you need to be in three years? In one year? What tasks will you have to have completed?

Work back from ten years to three years and then down to one year.

The action plans

So now you know where you want to go, why you are going there and what you need to do this year to get there. It is time then to break that down into the action steps you are going to take to make your must-dos a reality.

From your year plan, break down what tasks you will require to do to achieve your aims in a year. From there, break it down again into monthly, then a weekly plan. Once you have your weekly plan, you can clearly see what tasks will have to be done daily to reach your goals.

Note your daily tasks on your daily get-to-do list and voilà, you have a plan of action, ready for implementing. You can also add in any items from your general get-to-do list here to make sure those are being attended to.

Now this is the place for realism. There are only so many hours in a day and you are only one person. Fact. With that in mind, review your get-to-do list. Does it feel do-able? If not, go back and revise your plans – perhaps you need to have fewer aims. Review your aims: do you really want to achieve all of these things? If not, ship anything that isn't vital, or if you really must still have the item in your goals, park it for a bit on the bucket list and rest assured that you will get to it. Really dig into it all and only have things on your lists that are vital to you. Your time is so precious – use it wisely.

So now you have your Purposeful Action Plan in hand and are ready for action. Go you! Most people never take the time to sit down and make a Purposeful Action Plan and consequently they drift through life, never quite feeling fulfilled, never quite knowing what they really want, never quite achieving, never quite honouring their dreams. There is power in this process so well done you for completing it!

Review, review, review

Now that you have your Purposeful Action Plan and get-to-do list in hand, get to it. Get those tasks done. But don't be so busy doing that you lose sight of the bigger picture. Schedule a weekly planning meeting with yourself so you can sit down with your Purposeful Action Plan and check in with where you are at.

Ask yourself:

- Is everything on my Purposeful Action Plan still relevant to me?

- Am I on course? Do I need to change anything?

- What have I achieved this week – give yourself a huge pat on the back and really celebrate your achievement, because all too often we get caught up in the doing and don't take time to commend ourselves for our efforts and achievements

- What do I need to do this coming week to move forward towards my goals?

ACTION TAKER TASK: Write your get-to-do list down and get ready to roll for the coming week

PURPOSEFUL ACTION PLANNING

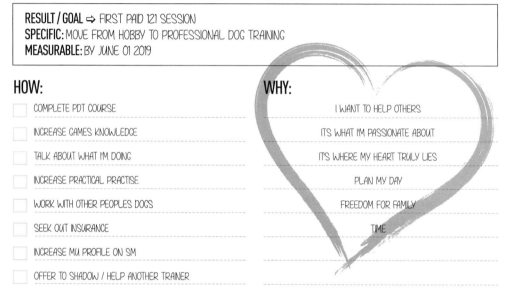

RESULT / GOAL ⇨ FIRST PAID 121 SESSION
SPECIFIC: MOVE FROM HOBBY TO PROFESSIONAL DOG TRAINING
MEASURABLE: BY JUNE 01 2019

HOW:

- ☐ COMPLETE PDT COURSE
- ☐ INCREASE GAMES KNOWLEDGE
- ☐ TALK ABOUT WHAT I'M DOING
- ☐ INCREASE PRACTICAL PRACTISE
- ☐ WORK WITH OTHER PEOPLES DOGS
- ☐ SEEK OUT INSURANCE
- ☐ INCREASE MY PROFILE ON SM
- ☐ OFFER TO SHADOW / HELP ANOTHER TRAINER

WHY:

I WANT TO HELP OTHERS

ITS WHAT I'M PASSIONATE ABOUT

IT'S WHERE MY HEART TRULY LIES

PLAN MY DAY

FREEDOM FOR FAMILY

TIME

RE-ENERGISE:

YOUR DEVELOPMENT:

ACTION TAKER'S PROGRESS

DAY PLAN
- ✔ To do
- ✘ Done
- ➤ Forward
- ✎ Cancel / Delete

DAY 1 PLAN
- ✔ LESSON 1-3 PDT
- ✔ 1 GAME TA
- ➤ PRACTISE WITH MY DOGS
- ✔ TELL 1 PERSON
- ✔ PODCAST/BOOK
- ✔ RE-ENERGISE

DAY 2 PLAN
- ✔ PRACTISE WITH MY DOGS
- ✔ LESSON 4/5
- ✔ 1 GAME TA
- ✔ TELL 1 PERSON
- ➤ VIDEO MY DOG TRAINING
- ☐

DAY 3 PLAN
- ✔ DAILY PLAN 3
- ☐ VIDEO
- ✔ ACTION TAKERS GUIDE
- ✔ 1 GAME TA
- ✔ PODCAST
- ✔ PICS ON FB

PURPOSEFUL ACTION PLANNING

RESULT / GOAL ⇨
SPECIFIC:
MEASURABLE:

HOW:

WHY:

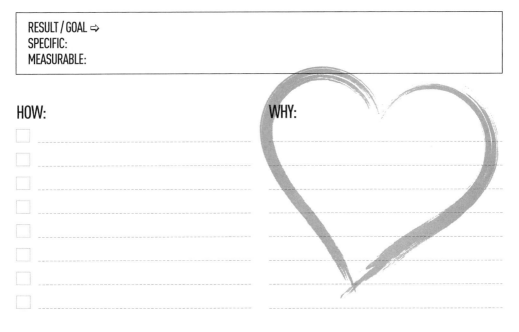

RE-ENERGISE:

YOUR DEVELOPMENT:

ACTION TAKER'S PROGRESS

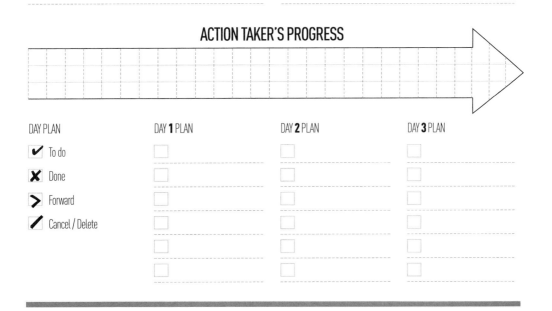

DAY PLAN

✔ To do
✘ Done
➤ Forward
✎ Cancel / Delete

DAY **1** PLAN

DAY **2** PLAN

DAY **3** PLAN

Also make time to check in with yourself daily – just quickly check in with yourself each evening on what you've achieved that day and what you need to achieve the following day. In the morning, refresh yourself on what you need to do, and then go for it.

Purposeful Action Planning reboot

Do a full review of your Purposeful Action Plan at least every six months to check in with yourself and make sure that everything is still true and relevant. Schedule time for this in your diary. It might feel like a luxury, but trust me, it is so necessary. You don't want to waste a single drop of your action taker energy going in a direction that isn't right for you.

The struggles with taking action

The beginning is the most important part of the work, and for all too many getting started is the very hardest part – analysis paralysis and action inertia are commonly seen in our world, especially when the project is not yet clear, and the journey is far from certain. That is a tough stage.

Completing your Purposeful Action Planning work is an amazing and powerful step. Once everything is laid out on paper and your plan has started to form, then it should be easy, right? Wrong. Just when you think you've got started and things are going forward, your brain catches on to what is happening and can very quickly put the brakes on in the form of *overwhelm*.

Overwhelm: The killer of great plans

Make no mistake, overwhelm can be a fearsome foe.

Starting a business, putting yourself out there into the world for all to see, and asking people to believe in your idea and come with you on a journey is massive. Your brain, which only ever wants to keep you safe, recognises this and throws up overwhelm as way to get you to beat a hasty retreat back into your comfort zone.

Taking positive action, even if it is just a tiny step, is key. The ability to step forward and move towards your goal or your vision is a big win. Remember, we are warriors. Whether it's a wisp of an idea or the big one, we must trust ourselves to make a decision and to make a move.

Starting a business is a huge task but it is certainly not insurmountable, no matter what your brain tries to tell you. The key to beating overwhelm is baby steps.

Taking baby steps

Starting a business is a lot of work, but it breaks down very easily into a lot of small, easy steps.

For example:

Start a dog training business -> find a suitable venue for classes -> do a Google search of local churches, community halls, training fields -> prepare a list of possible venues -> contact the venues and make enquires

Or

Start a dog training business -> get business insurance -> research business insurance providers -> plan what cover you will need -> work out your budget for the policy -> contact providers to get quotes -> choose best quote -> purchase policy

Don't try to do everything at once

Of course, breaking everything down into baby steps does not completely fool your brain into believing that everything is rosy and that it can stand down from danger mode. Your brain will still be very aware that it has many small but manageable tasks to manage and that thought itself can cause overwhelm.

To deal with this, be realistic about the number of tasks you are able to do in a day. You will not be able to do everything. This is especially true if you are setting up your dog business as a side hustle at the start.

A good rule of thumb is to pick the top three tasks on your get-to-do list that must be done that day and make sure that those get done. If you can't manage three per day, just make sure you do at least one to keep things moving forward each day. If you manage all three and have time and energy left, you can choose another item from your get-to-do list.

Steady completion of your baby steps will quickly add up to getting a lot done and before you know it, you will have serious momentum to take your business forward.

ACTION TAKER TASK: What three get-to-do list tasks can you do today?

1:

2:

3:

My goal is to progress the business, just a little, each day. A little will become a lot very quickly.

Nathan Leighton, Gamechanger

Be a doer of great things

When we step forward, it can initially throw us off balance, even just a little. Be patient with and kind to yourself. Heading into the unknown can be tough. Harness that magical combination of fear and excitement to drive you forward and have the courage to know that there is a way. Put your passion and your heart in the only direction that truly matters, which is, as you already know, forward: heart and mind forward, get in the arena, dare greatly and stand up, show up.

Tips for taking action

Two things will turbo charge your dog business success:

1. Self-awareness

2. Consistency in action

1. Self-awareness

Self-awareness is critical to improvement. It is key to identifying where things are working well and where they could use a little tweaking, to why things are working and why they are not. Observe yourself. If you find yourself with too much to do and too little time, keep a record of how you spend your day. Be brutally honest. No one needs to read it but you. Write down everything you do for two weeks, then analyse your findings. Don't judge – just observe, note and reflect. Did everything you want to do make it onto your timesheet? What was left out? Were all of your tasks urgent? Were they important? Really scrutinise what is on there and use that list to plan what should go into your days going forward and what you would prefer to do less of.

If you are going to fill a jar with rocks, pebbles, sand and water, you have to put the rocks in first. If you fill it with any of the others first, you will not be able to fit the rocks in. The rocks are the tasks that are most important to you, but often get pushed out of your diary by smaller, more urgent matters. Put the rocks in first.

2. Consistency in action

If you don't move, you won't get anywhere. It is as simple as that. Taking a step every day will move you along the road and will begin to create momentum. It also builds your confidence. So don't stay stuck in planning or busywork: put your best foot forward and take that step. Then do the same tomorrow. And the next day. And the next.

Top tips for taking action

Struggling to get going? Here are some top tips to prompt you into action:

- Get a great sleep – you will need a clear head and good energy levels for the entrepreneur journey.

- Get your key tasks scheduled into your day first and make them habits – include the things you love doing and the things you should be doing.

- Work smarter, not harder. Be super aware of how you spend your time. Always ask 'why am I doing this?' If you don't know, stop doing it.

- Be flexible. There is enough time – it is just how you use it that can work against you. Watch your energy and your attitude. Don't use phrases such as 'I'm so busy' or 'I don't have enough time'. You create your own reality, so don't create that sort of life.

- Prioritise your important tasks and make sure they don't get overtaken by the urgent tasks.

- Get an early start. It is amazing how much you can get done in the quiet hours before the world wakes.

- If something is unpleasant to do, commit to doing it. Some people find they have to make tasks even more unpleasant to motivate them to move, for example, leaving their tax returns until the deadline day. If something is so unpleasant, ask yourself whether you should be doing it at all. Can it be dropped or delegated? If not, find a way to make it more pleasant – pair it with something you enjoy, such as having a cup of tea, or meeting up with a friend after it. Commit to doing it and get it off your get-to-do list as soon as possible. By leaving it, you only suffer for longer.

- Watch for time sinks. Everyone has at some point lifted their phone to check for messages and then wondered where the last hour went. Social media, idle Messenger chats, scrolling through the news, it all adds up. Be aware.

- Aim for progress, not perfection.

- Give yourself time for tasks – you will get way more done, you will stay more focused and you will supercharge your work.

- Exercise – it doesn't have to be an exhausting, gruelling workout to do you good. A gentle ten-minute walk will do. Just get moving. You'll feel the benefit.

- Experiment with your routines – we tend to adopt routines, especially those we grew up with, so try new ways of doing things. Shake it up and see if you can find new approaches that work for you.

- Give yourself permission to have buffer time. Take a bath or a shower, do some exercise, go for a walk, meditate – allow yourself time to reset and recharge. You are not a machine and cannot expect to work constantly and continuously without allowing yourself any downtime. Take ten, then come back fresh and ready to give your best to the world.

Reclaimed time

If you are really looking to get efficient with your day, use reclaimed time. Use your time more consciously and wisely. If you are commuting, don't read the newspaper. Answer emails instead. Don't scroll through Facebook; write and post a new advert for your business. Taking your dog to the vet? Take the opportunity to speak to the receptionist about your new dog walking business while you are there.

There is always a way to make the most of the time you have. Those times when you zone out or aren't intentionally using your time are usually gems of possibility for getting tasks that will move your business forward.

Don't take other people's urgents

People love to dump urgent tasks. Urgent tasks can be so uncomfortable that people will take great joy in launching them into the hands of the nearest willing, or even unwilling, recipient. It doesn't matter what these monster urgents-bearing offloaders tell you: their urgent task is not your responsibility – unless you choose to make it your responsibility. If you choose to do so, having carefully considered where it is necessary and appropriate for you to do so, then that is fine. Take the task with intention and get on with getting it done.

But if that urgent task is not for you, should not be done or dealt with by you, or will greatly impact on your other tasks, then you have the right to say no. In fact, you have the duty to say no. You owe it to yourself, your life and that other person to say no. Being the person who always says yes teaches other people that it is ok to dump last-minute or short-notice tasks on you. That does not teach the offloader anything about managing their own time and responsibilities.

It might feel good to help bail someone out, but you are likely to get resentful. That can lead to you not completing the task to the best of your ability. Put boundaries in place and don't accept urgent tasks without fully considering first whether it is appropriate for you to do the task and second whether you even should do the task. Just because you can doesn't mean you should.

Just say no

Practise saying no. It might sound crazy but having a few stock phrases for declining tasks or invitations ready to roll off your tongue will save you when you are faced with imminently agreeing to something that you don't want to do.

Key phrases such as 'thank you for thinking of me, but I can't make it. I've got something else on that day' or 'I'd love to be involved with that, but I just don't have the capacity to take anything else on at the minute' are a polite but firm way to decline invitations without causing offence.

Don't waffle. Don't apologise. And don't feel like you have to explain yourself. You do not owe anyone an explanation for saying no. They have every right to ask you to do something, but you also always retain the right to say no.

Fools rush in

If you need time to think about a request, ask for it. Advise the person that you will check your diary, or that you will consider it and get back to them. No one has the right to an instant response. Consider the invitation and then get back to the person as promptly as possible with your decision.

Be brave

Tell me, what is it you plan to do with your one wild and precious life?

Mary Oliver

Those who are brave are free. Be *brave*. Conformity is the jailer of our freedom and the enemy of growth. Connecting with who we really are will allow growth and minimise fear. We shall meet life with our full presence and power. Be brave. Always be brave.

We all have those goals, those dreams that burn inside and deep down you know that's who you are, and what you are meant to do and want to achieve, your inner purpose, your inner desire. But often we don't make that leap because we are scared of taking the risk, that jump, scared of what might be, what could happen, what could change. Fear can be crippling. But for me, fear is always a sign that something matters to me.

Taking the leap

Things started to become so busy that a decision had to be made, it was a leap of faith, to put full-time effort into my new business. This was an incredibly scary and daunting position to be in, giving up a regular income for the complete unknown!

Nikki Thurston, Gamechanger

Making a big life change can be pretty scary, but you know what's scarier? Regret or living a life wishing you had given it a shot. And regret can last a life time. We rarely regret the things we do – it is usually the things we didn't do. Remember, the greatest sadness and pain we will ever see in our lives are from people who have spent their lives outside the arena wondering what would or could have happened if they had just stepped inside.

I remember taking the leap so well. I was teaching English and law to 11–18 year olds. I was in a performance review and I was offered the position of head of year during the interview. In that very moment I knew that I was capable, I knew that it was a well-paid job offer, I knew I could make a difference and I knew that it was a very good opportunity for me professionally. But in that moment I realised that it was not my opportunity, and in that situation following my dreams was the only option. I knew that I needed to be brave.

I not only declined the very kind and generous job offer, but I also handed in my notice. I would no longer work as a teacher. I was going to run my own business. I wanted to explore my passion, I wanted more freedom and I wanted to contribute. And that job as a school teacher just didn't cut it.

Have you ever felt that? Does any of this resonate with you? Can you relate to any of this? I was scared, for sure. I felt massive fear and vulnerability, but so much stronger than the feeling of fear was the desire to fight for freedom, for passion and for what I desired. That is a very powerful and deep why. I chose to fight.

How can you change anything in your life? How do you get what you want? Is it even possible to break down the blocks, smash down the walls? What are your goals and crazy dreams? What are your hopes and what is your passion? What are you scared of? People begin to become truly successful the minute they let go of fear and they truly decide to be successful.

ACTION TAKER TASK: List all of your blocks so you can smash them. What is keeping you from your passion? What can you do to overcome these? Really get creative on this. You never know what crazy brainwave might hold the key to breaking down a huge barrier.

Hope, confidence, bravery, passion and creativity will take you forward. Go smash those roadblocks.

THE ROADBLOCK REFRAME

DREAM VISION	OBSTACLE	REFRAME	ACTION
DOG TRAINER	I DON'T HAVE THE RIGHT QUALIFICATION	I WILL COMPLETE THE PDT COURSE	SIGN UP FOR PRO DOG TRAINER
	MY KNOWLEDGE ISN'T GOOD ENOUGH	I WILL TAKE ACTION PUT INTO PRACTICE	START TO GET PRACTICAL EXPERIENCE
	I CAN'T AFFORD TO DO IT	WHERE CAN I SAVE WHAT CAN I SELL HOW CAN I GENERATE	PUT THE CASH TOWARDS MY OWN PERSONAL DEVELOPMENT

THE ROADBLOCK REFRAME

YOUR TURN...

DREAM VISION	OBSTACLE	REFRAME	ACTION

When you are stuck in the 'doing'

It can be tough starting something new. Dreams get replaced with firefighting, busy days, crazy busy days, a complete lack of time and a hundred other reasons not to spend time doing what we truly want to. Finances can be a struggle and utilising energy correctly on you can seem like an impossibility. When that gets lost, we really are in big trouble. But, the real question is, how do we get back on track?

That's where the Time Travel game comes in.

ACTION TAKER TASK: The Time Travel game

Get out your answers to the Your Powerful Why task in Chapter 1. Read them through and really feel them. Remember what it felt like when you were completing that task, the optimism and energy you felt then, the drive to go forward. Let those feelings fill you up, let them charge your energy.

Then, consult your plan and get-to-do list from the Purposeful Action Planning task earlier in this chapter. What is the easiest practical step you can take next to move things forward? Feel the energy of your powerful why fill you up and then go for it.

Fear shies from the light of action. You will always feel better if you do something. So travel through time, rejuvenate your energy, then get going.

Put yourself out there

Business is all about creation: creating products and services, wealth, opportunity. The act of creating a buzz around your business can be one of the most fun parts of building a business. Talking about your business and seeing people's eyes light up (in person or online as they like and join your social media pages) as they recognise the value in what you are bringing to the world and realise that it could make a difference to them, as they grab the torch and take it forward, to take your message out even further to the world, gives goosebumps indeed. It is making a difference at its most fundamental. And it feels awesome.

So if you have an idea for a business, talk to people about it. Ask relevant people if they would be interested in using your product or service. You'll find out many things you didn't know. You will challenge assumptions you have made about your customers, demand and what your customers will look for in your product or service, and you will begin to create a buzz around your business even before you have opened the doors.

And once your business is up and running? Never stop talking about it. Be brave, be bold and get talking. People need to know you exist. You have built a product or service to meet a need – the people with that need must be told about you. If you have something that can help someone, why would you keep quiet about it? You serve no one by hiding your light under a bushel, so get out there and shine.

> *When you know you have something special to offer, and you know that what you teach can truly make a difference to dogs and their owners, and you know the world needs more positive dog trainers, you soon realise it's not about having a purpose-built venue, the latest matching equipment or the newest gadget. Everything can be achieved simply, cheaply and the fancy stuff can wait. You just need to get started.*
>
> Sarah Jane McLaren, Gamechanger

Always marketing

You are a walking, talking business card. You are a living, breathing piece of marketing material. In every interaction you have, you have the opportunity to represent and promote your business. Do not be shy.

Think outside the box: if you have a dog walking business, instead of just putting flyers in the waiting room of your local vet practice, could you do an information evening for their clients on the importance of exercise to keeping your dog healthy? Could you do a talk for your local Rotary Club on starting a side hustle business? Rather than simply looking to promote your business, seek to tell your story. Humans buy from humans and humans buy stories, so tell your story and the story of your business, rather than always looking to cut straight to the sale.

ACTION TAKER TASK: Talk to ten people this week about your business. Five of them must be strangers.

BUSINESS CHAT
WHO DID YOU SPREAD THE WORD TO?

KNOWN	WHO	THEIR RESPONSE
1		
2		
3		
4		
5		

UNKNOWN	WHO	THEIR RESPONSE
1		
2		
3		
4		
5		

The biggest challenge is marketing. I am surrounded by some amazing training locations that offer a variety of services. I must make myself stand out, and word of mouth is really essential to growth. It is important to do the foot work, to take the steps to reach out and develop a relationship with compatible services, such as veterinary clinics and grooming locations. These are the people who will be recommending you and it is important to have a positive connection with them and to maintain that relationship professionally.

Dana Escobar, Gamechanger

Don't be afraid to do things differently

The world needs creative solutions to its problems. Never be frightened to solve a problem in a new way or to do something differently. Be an innovator, a disruptor. Change the way things have always been done and blaze a new trail.

Creativity in our dog businesses is vital. Why?

1. Creativity is essential for solving complex problems – the kind we often find in a fast paced-world.

2. Creativity gives you a competitive edge. Attempts to train people to be more creative are often not terribly successful. Why? We are trying to train a skill but what we are really trying to achieve is a state of mind. And what is that state of mind? The solution seeker state of mind, of course.

So, you solution seeking Gamechanger, get out there and rewrite the rules!

This is the fastest it has ever been and the slowest it will ever be. That is why we love disruptors.

Sir Tom Hunter

Create an alter ego

If you are really struggling with putting yourself out there, having an alter ego can help. Creating your own innovative superhero is both a fun and empowering way to enable you to supercharge your chances of success. You don't have to don Lycra – just giving yourself that name or adopting a role moves you closer to that model and it is who you will become.

Those simple words can change your whole perception of an event, action, task or to do item. For example, in my house my mum has often called me the Golden Goose. That identity change changes my role, how I feel and how I focus on my role. The child-like emotions that I feel when I am the Golden Goose helps to supercharge me through the challenges, and makes it easier for me to reach those goals.

ACTION TAKER TASK: Create your alter ego

YOU

YOUR NAME:

ALTER EGO NAME:

Focus

Focus is a secret superpower. It is a seriously underrated ability in this age of distraction in which we live, but you will find that most successful people have it and those who don't have someone in their close team who do and can keep them on track.

In addition to the normal, everyday distractions posed by our always connected world, there are always a million distractions ready and waiting in your business to pull you away from what needs to be done. Resist the temptation. It can be so tempting to indulge in busywork, work that feels urgent and important but in fact is neither. Don't succumb.

Know what you are doing

Always be aware of how you are spending your time and ask yourself 'is this really worth my time?' That goes for recreational time use as well. Knowing what you are doing and why are key to managing your days and getting everything done that needs to be done. If you have carefully chosen what you are doing with your time, you are free to concentrate on it fully and freely, knowing that it is the most appropriate use of your time or, if not, that at least you know that and are choosing to do it.

The 80/20 rule

The Pareto principle, or 80/20 rule as it is also known, provides that around 80% of your achievement will come from around 20% of your effort. It is therefore super important to prioritise and to focus like laser on the 20% items that are likely to generate your 80% results. The other, less important items can wait.

Practise, practise, practise

Practise focusing in everything that you do. If you are reading, researching or writing, don't pick up your phone and quickly check emails or social media. If you are talking with someone, don't have the television on or pick up your phone. Always look for opportunities to be present in the moment.

Focus on your tasks until they are complete and resist the urge to jump to another task or distraction. Focus is like a muscle – you have to work on it to make it strong. If you manage this, you will set yourself so far ahead of most of our chronically distracted society.

Urgent versus important

In a world that does its best to make you think that everything has to be done *right now* and actively encourages fractured focus and frenzied activity, how can you work out what needs to be done in a day? What deserves your time and what can you ditch?

President Dwight D. Eisenhower was known for his time management skills. He once quoted someone in a speech saying there are "two kinds of problems, the urgent and the important. The urgent are not important, and the important are never urgent."

This became known as the Eisenhower Principle and is a useful tool for deciding how to spend your time.

Accordingly, your tasks will fall into four categories. These are ranked in order of priority, with category 1 being the highest priority, and category 4 being the lowest.

1. Important and urgent

In category 1, you are dealing with tasks that are important to you so that should be fun, right? Unfortunately, that is often not the case: category 1 are often time bound and a deadline looms. These items need your attention now and rank highest in the priority list, so they have the ability to knock lower ranked tasks off your schedule.

This is fine if something comes up that is unavoidably urgent. But if you are spending all of your time dealing with category 1 items to the detriment of other items on your get-to-do list, it can be a sign that you are not scheduling your tasks properly. The category that is hardest hit by this is often your category 2 tasks, so beware.

2. Important but not urgent

In this category are the things that really matter. You are investing in yourself in category 2. This is the creative zone and it's the most fun place to be. This is where you are investing in yourself and doing what matters most to you. Unfortunately, despite being the second highest priority, it is also the place we are least likely to spend time because the other categories tend to call more loudly for our attention.

Category 2 items need planning and regular attention. These items are way more fun to do in a timely manner. Plan, prepare and do the work ahead of time: get these items done before people are looking for them. If you fail to schedule in work on your category 2 items, they will either become category 1 important and urgent and not nearly as much fun to deal with, or they will fade away completely and be lost. So put them on your radar screen, schedule time for them and make them happen.

3. Not important but urgent

These items have a deadline, but are they the best use of your time? If you are doing something that isn't important to you, you really need to question whether you should be doing it at all. Can you delegate these tasks?

Category 3 tasks are particularly dangerous because they command your attention through their urgency and can easily muscle your category 2 tasks off your list. You will be busy and feel like you are doing something when you have category 3 tasks on your to-do list but they are not the right things. They are unlikely to be moving you in the direction of your dreams.

4. Not important and not urgent

Anything that takes up your time but gives you very little in return belongs in category 4. Mindless scrolling on social media, watching random videos, playing games on your phone for lengthy periods, anything that makes you feel zoned out falls into category 4. Chilling and taking down time are very important but be intentional about them and put appropriate time for them in your schedule – they are category 2 items. If you lift your phone when you should be attending to important items, then you are in the realm of category 4. Ditch these activities and use the time you've freed up for category 2 activities.

Be careful not to put tasks in this category just because they are fun. Like relaxation, fun is important and thus belongs in category 2.

I know that from everything we have learned on the courses that I need to work out what is important, what is urgent, what is not important and what is not urgent. I know what I need to do, but not important urgent things often land in front of me making my life a little bit topsy-turvy. Work in progress!

Vicky Mansfield, Gamechanger

CHAPTER 10

WHO REACHES OUT AND GRABS REAL-LIFE RESULTS

The man in the arena

It is not the critic who counts; not the man who points out how the strong man stumbles, or where the doer of deeds could have done them better. The credit belongs to the man who is actually in the arena, whose face is marred by dust and sweat and blood; who strives valiantly; who errs, who comes short again and again, because there is no effort without error and shortcoming; but who does actually strive to do the deeds; who knows great enthusiasms, the great devotions; who spends himself in a worthy cause; who at the best knows in the end the triumph of high achievement, and who at the worst, if he fails, at least fails while daring greatly, so that his place shall never be with those cold and timid souls who neither know victory nor defeat.

Theodore Roosevelt

Becoming an action taker

I am an action taker. I love being an action taker. It is thrilling, exciting, defining and exhilarating at every level. I am always the one in the arena, and most of the time I'm smiling. I'm really grinning from ear to ear.

Get into the arena

Right now not only have I got two very happy, confident pooches, but I am so much happier myself and I feel my confidence is improving every day – something I have struggled with in the past. I'm in the middle of negotiating premises that will make my dream a reality. I am so excited about the future!

Sam Paxton, Gamechanger

Truly being an action taker is built on a foundation of so many of the concepts and elements we have discussed in this book: growth mindset, powerful why, solution seeking, great team building. All of these equal the true ability to be real-life action taker.

And what an incredible place to be, a truly remarkable, an outstanding place – are you in the arena, are you ready to play all out? There is only one definitive answer, and it's a 'hell yeah!' You are here; you are present.

Don't be a spectator

Dreams don't work unless you do.

John C. Maxwell

One of the very saddest things we will ever see in our lives is someone outside the arena, watching, wishing, waiting, hoping and wondering what would or could have happened if they had simply stood up, made a move and actually shown up. Or being the critic, watching and criticising the person trying and striving valiantly.

Go all in

Are you in the arena? Really and truly? Not just thinking about it, dreaming about it, planning it? Is there dust on your shoes? It is time to ascend to another level of existence. Be ready to declare your personal power, freedom and joy. Be ready to get your hands, feet and face dirty and to love it. There is no better place to be than in the arena, wrestling with life and forging your own destiny.

*My advice to anyone starting up a business of any scale is
to do it. There is never a good time, there is never going
to be that bank balance we all want to get started. There
are a million reasons not to but there are so many
million more reasons to say yes. You are amazing and
you can do this.*

Becky Beacock, Gamechanger

Things I wish I had known when I started out

*Now is no time to think of what you do not have. Think of
what you can do with what there is.*

Ernest Hemingway

1. You don't have to be perfect. Society leads us down a path where we
believe that if we look a certain way, dress a certain way, and act and speak
in certain way then we will be more accepted, we will fit in, we will be
loved more and we will have community, and until we are perfect sometimes we should wait, or not try.

   Well, getting started is the exact opposite of that. We have been brain-
washed to strive for perfection and all of this striving for the impossible,
the unreachable and the untouchable can make us pretty miserable.
Having goals is healthy, but perfection isn't. It steals our joy.

   So getting started is *not* about perfection. It's about making a start. When I
first started, I did not have a venue, I did not have a guaranteed income, I
knew nothing about running a business. But I was keen, passionate, and
had huge desire and a mission, and I was getting started. I was in the arena
and I was fighting hard.

2. Have a niche. Be bold, stand out, be different. Standing out came early in
my dog career. I realised that there were simply loads of trainers around so
I really needed to stand out. I visited loads of other clubs, I watched
lessons, I took my own dogs, Bella and Popi, to various lessons. I noted
things I could adapt and things I could make more bespoke. I looked at

niche areas. I didn't want to step on anyone's toes and I needed to stand out. So here are a few of the changes I made after being in various similar training scenarios:

- No chairs at my classes – I wanted students to be on the go. I wanted them to move and to be able to enjoy their whole lesson and not to sit down and wait patiently for their turn.

- I would welcome naughty dogs. Little did I know they would become one of our biggest specialist areas. We now fondly know of this niche group of dogs and owners as 'Naughty But Nice'.

- I would have beds, boundaries and crates at training and encourage students and dogs to use them. They would become an integral part of our classes and later became known as Boundary Games.

- Students would take an active role in setting up, teaching and packing down the class. I realised (from my teacher training) that it was imperative for students and their dogs to build the games, the ideas and the class community right from the very beginning. I also realised that so many regular school teachers burn out and that was not something I was willing to accept. So these thoughts were implemented pretty much from the outset.

- To allow classes to run long term and to facilitate future learning, I decided from the outset that we would have an online booking system and would book lessons in blocks. From observing other classes, I quickly realised that the time spent collecting the class money was a pain point for both the owner and the teacher, and it also really ate in to the super precious class time; therefore my classes would be pre-booked and block booked.

- My lessons would be differentiated, meaning that I would have mixed ability groups for the majority of my classes and I would adjust the lesson as I needed and therefore avoid competitive cliques and groups within classes. It would also enable more effective goal setting and would prove all in all to be a great advantage to all classes, students and instructors.

There were so many observations and unique points I wanted to bring into my own classes. On the whole, we've maintained most of the adaptations. So many at the time were very unique to dog training classes and I'm happy to say that, 15 years on, many other clubs and trainers have taken these ideas on and they have moved on again to another level.

3. Build a strong, dedicated and caring community in all that you do. Use social media, face-to-face meet-ups, posters, virtual mail-outs, physical mail-outs – whatever it takes to get your community and your tribe off the ground and started. But always stay true to your values and true to yourself. It really doesn't matter what the business is; what matters most is how it's conducted and who is the community behind it. Whether you are dog grooming, walking, training or doing physio, having the community's passion, love and understanding behind what you do is vital for success. Grow and love your tribe.

We like to think of it as magnets: attract the people you want around what you do and make sure that they know you enjoy them and their dogs and always make sure that they are valued. Treat them as you would want to be treated and grow the passion for what you do together and build that feeling of worth. Reward loyalty, have a recommend-a-friend scheme, grow regular referrals to what you do via your community and enjoy like-minded people. I think it's always possible to inspire your community, increase their confidence, make sure they know they are appreciated, help them to connect to others and push them to challenge themselves where they would like to grow.

4. Have faith in the Universe and in yourself. I remember right at the very beginning, my mentor, Michael, said, "Lauren, if you build it, they will come – you are a strong magnet. Trust the Universe; they will come." And he was right, I built it and they came. So whether we are talking about, as in my case, a venue, or whether we are talking about the idea in principle once you have sounded it out, I truly believe in the saying build it and they will come.

5. The number one rule is ... there are no rules. There really are no rules. Be ready to get on board, get great at decision making and be decisive, don't wobble, procrastinate or overthink. Most of the time, whatever you

decided is 100% right anyway. Make the decision and then work out what needs to be done.

Get even better at making things happen and add motivation and momentum at every stage. The key is to find the dynamism in yourself to lead what you are doing in a changing world. This will bring complete business success and launch your business to the next level.

Remember, always, that you are a force of nature and remember that things can change in a moment. Stay true to your beliefs and values, get emotionally connected and committed and always, always risk moving ahead.

Killing a job as you know it

I went from being a school teacher, with the feeling that I was in a huge pressure cooker, to another role, with equally huge persuasion and influence but with a whole new emotional feeling, a whole new league of passion and a completely different energy. In the early days of starting my first business, Devon Dogs, it was like truly finding myself. It was like coming home.

I'm a gambler and a risk taker, so walking away from a fairly large salary with reliability and clear guarantees wasn't so difficult for me. However, I know for some people this is huge, but when you run your own business you design your days. And this is priceless.

And that leads us back to our powerful why. It all comes back to your deep-rooted beliefs, headspace and values, because when you are running your own business you become far more emotionally committed than ever before. And being able to come up with novel ideas, games, strategies and plans is key to achieving success in running your own successful and efficient business.

Embrace the side hustle

If leaving your current employment is not a possibility, there is always the option to start your dog business as a side hustle. Smartphones have made it easier than ever to work on your business at any time. Use every moment you have to work on your business: during your commute, at lunchtime, once the kids are in bed.

If you can, get a job that facilitates working on your dream, for example, working nights so you can be free for client appointments during the day, or working during the day so you can run training classes in the evening – whatever works for your dog business. Just always make sure that you leverage your skills to get the best paid role you can that works with what you need. Also consider the possibility of reducing your hours in your current employment to allow time to work on your dog business.

Building a side hustle alongside your current employment is not a bad place to be. Knowing that your bills will be paid every month reduces the fear that can prove overwhelming. Desperation is never a great place to come from, practically or energetically. You can have fun building your side hustle, trying things out and testing your business model.

You will know when the time is right to leave your day job and go full time in your hustle: when your income from your side hustle can support you and you require all your time to fulfil the needs of your business. Then it is time to ditch the day job and go all in.

> *I never did a day's work in my life. It was all fun.*
>
> Thomas Edison

The hard times

Okay, I'm not going to paint this pretty picture and fool you into thinking that it's all pink and fluffy. There will be the odd testing situation or scenario to consider in any dog business. Below are just a few that I have come across over my time in business – and I'm sure you can add a few more to the list. But remember there is always a game for that (whether it be a human one or a dog training one):

- Finding venues . . . enough said, it can be tough.

- The weather – it's too hot, too cold, too snowy. . .the list goes on.

- Your venue – there is an issue with the venue and a neighbour.

- Financial struggle – it is just not making ends meet.

- Staff or lack of staff issue – should you take someone on? Should you let someone go?

- Planning permission

- Confidence with other similar businesses close by

- Sickness or illness or time off or holidays…who will run the business when you aren't there? What can you do to help grow this?

Running a dog business is for sure not a nine-to-five job, and there are boundaries to establish to allow you to maintain a balanced and happy life. But to wake up each day knowing that you love the life you live, and that you truly live the life you love, is very special. Finding solutions to the tough days and struggles as well as enjoying the lighter days in balance is key.

Not everything you want to do will be well supported. You will meet road blocks and you will need huge amounts, bucket loads some days, of commitment and persistence to strive for exactly what you desire. There will be many people, restrictions, enforcements and regulations that can potentially get in your way. Overcoming obstacles with true presence and power is part of the roller coaster, and what doesn't kill you keeps you alive. It's all part of the thrill, right? The highs and the lows.

I knew somehow the money would come and I took the leap of faith that as long as I followed my dream, my passion, I would be ok. And I was.

Teri Thomas, Gamechanger

Cut yourself some slack

Often we will put off starting things until we are 'perfect' at them. Remember that perfection is an illusion, an unattainable mirage – and who would want to be left with no room still to grow? Perfection is for people who believe in the destination, rather than the journey. Such people are not Gamechangers.

So give yourself permission to be flawed, to make mistakes. No one starts in a sport expecting to know all the rules, moves, techniques and quirks at the outset; why do we do it to ourselves in life and in business? Cut yourself some slack and be prepared to make mistakes. Heck, welcome them. They give you valuable feedback and an opportunity for learning and growth. Mastery only comes through practice, so get out there and *do*!

The joy of not following the prescribed path

So 15 years on from turning down the opportunity to be in the legal world, I walked into a local solicitor's office. We had to do some land ownership paper-work after purchasing a small piece of land close to Bowerland. To cut a very long story short, I walked out so very grateful, so very relieved. I walked out alive, I walked out knowing that, in every single bone in my body, in every muscle, in every fibre, that my life was so very much more meaningful to me in terms of my personal passion, desire and intent than it could have been had I not followed my dream.

I made that step some 15 years ago to leave the 'successful' position, to move to a world of uncertainty. But now I am so very certain, more than ever, that I live in joy and happiness and passion and excitement, and I know this can be the case for you too. Success is defined and measured in so many different ways, but mostly for me in the measure of happiness, and how you feel within, when who you are meets what you do. And in doing what we love most, we are not only truly happy, but truly privileged every single day.

> *Stop being afraid of what could go wrong, and start being excited of what could go right.*
>
> Tony Robbins

Imitation is the sincerest form of flattery

> *Today you are you, that is truer than true. There is no one alive who is you-er than you.*
>
> Dr Seuss

On a very quick note, one thing that I have had to work through and consider for sure is never to be upset if someone copies you. After all, no one truly invented all of this. We are simply redesigning it for our own purposes and needs. We can share and we can grow.

Also, remind yourself of your powerful why. For most of us, that's happier and healthier dogs and their owners worldwide, so actually if people want to mirror you, that's likely to mean dogs surrounding them and all around the world will be benefitting from those great ideas you had. How cool is that? Other people spreading your great words, your tools, your games and your solutions. They are going to help dogs worldwide.

The key thing that will set you apart, and the thing that no one else has, is *being you*. You are special indeed. There is no one else in this world with precisely the same knowledge, experience, thoughts, hopes, dreams, talents and abilities that you have. You came here to fulfil a special mission and no one – no one - can replicate that or do it for you. So no matter how hard someone tries, they will never be able to capture that essence that makes your work your own.

Just keep doing your thing. Trust in abundance, know that your people will come to you and be certain that you are making a massive difference.

> *Before going it alone, know your market, who your customers are, how you are going to reach them and have your unique selling point so people choose you rather than competitors. This can be skills, this can be packaging, whatever you decide – be awesome!*
>
> Alex Wilson, Gamechanger

CHAPTER 11

AND NEVER (NEVER) STOP TRANSFORMING THROUGH GAMES

Never (never) stop transforming through games

Play is the highest form of research.

Neville V. Scarfe

We are not done; we are never done. So this really is not the end; this is just the beginning. This is your first introduction to the Pro Dog Trainer community, so your eyes have been opened to the innovation, the creativity, the support and the vibrancy of the absoluteDogs world and community and the world that is available to you in starting up and maintaining your dog business.

Always be ready to bounce back, always stand right back up, always shake it off and never, never ever quit. It all begins and ends in your mind: what you give power to has power over you, if you choose to allow it. Take opportunities again and again and never, never stop transforming through games.

When I let go of who I am, I become what I might be.

Lao Tzu

Find your niche

The key is for sure to find your niche, your special area, your area of passion and drive. What do you find most fun? What do you do differently? For our team, at absoluteDogs HQ, Naughty But Nice was definitely an area to grow. Nobody wanted to tackle that area and we actively loved it, felt passionate about it, nurtured and grew it. It was our baby and we wanted to look after it and see it change the dog ownership world. We wanted Naughty But Nice dogs lives to change worldwide.

The reach has blown me away, and the difference it has made to dogs, and dog owners lives around the world is huge. It is not only hugely satisfying but also very fulfilling from a job satisfaction point of view when you see how happy dogs and their owners are. NBN rocks and the NBN movement is global.

Are you ready to run your own business?

So we move this directly on to you, is it right for you, running your own business? After all, the role of personality has to come in somewhere.

So, running a business is, for me, a little like getting to eat chocolate cake every day. It is completely addictive, it tastes great, it's moreish and for sure there are some huge advantages. So let's start with those, the very best bits:

1. You run your diary and find your own balance

2. You choose your clients

3. You can dictate the amount of work you add to your day

4. You control the income and salaries and cash flow

5. You can work as hard as you like

6. You can pick your team and who you work with

7. You have flexibility in the work place

8. You control your destiny

9. You reap the rewards

10. You follow your passion and challenge yourself

> *Your smile is your logo, your personality is your business card. How you leave others feeling after having an experience with you becomes your trademark.*
>
> Jay Danzie

The struggles

On the flip side, running your own business does have the odd struggle to contend with and I know we have touched on a few of these:

1. Financial risk is obviously down to you and income will fluctuate as that's the very nature of business – and the lack of income predictability can be unsettling

2. Business owners tend to have more stress and health-related issues

3. There is more commitment

4. It's all up to you – decisions, decisions...

5. Lines can become very blurred and the work-life balance can become diffi-cult to maintain

6. Your clients are your boss, sometimes they really are in charge

7. Employees . . . enough said.

8. You spend your own money, so when you need something new it's a whole new decision-making process – and it hurts that little bit more

9. You earn what you earn

10. You find it very hard to be away from your business, so holidays and other commitments can be very tough

> *For me being a Gamechanger and Pro Dog Trainer isn't just about getting success with dogs. It isn't about the end goal or getting that behaviour. It's more about inspiring owners, other trainers and people to be kind, enjoy the journey and have fun with their dogs in anyway they can – whether that be playing middle as recall, orientation to inspire good choices or just playing fitness games at home because they've had a tough day and can't face the world in that moment. It's about being flexible with expectations, routes to progression and life with a dog.*
>
> Chris Jackman, Gamechanger

Is running a business for you?

Is running a business for everyone? Possibly not. However, my guess is that since you have read this far, you are all in. Or maybe you are reading for the person who runs the business you work in, and maybe they are so deeply wrapped up in entrepreneurship that they can't possibly tear themselves away to read this book and you are the dream employee, the employee who strives to do more, to be bigger, to reach higher and yet doesn't want to have a business but wants to be part of that bigger and higher purpose. Heck, if so, I want to employ you.

Business planning and general day-to-day running for sure has its ups and downs, but I can't remember the last down day to date, and I can tell you all of the up days. So I'm going to stick my neck out and say doing what you love rocks, and being part of something that makes a difference, that makes your heart beat a little faster, takes your breath away and allows you to leap out of bed with a spring in your step is for sure worth it. I have never, ever regretted once leaving my salaried employment. Not even once. And I cannot ever imagine going back to that world. Never . . . ever.

> *My training school has been running for a year now and it has been the best year of my life so far. I love that I can design my day and I am in control of what I do and how I choose to spend my time. I love the flexibility running my own training school brings. I love that I can share my passion and spread the awesome message that there are far better ways to train! I love the smiles on my students' faces when they are seeing success on their own journeys. Being in charge of my own destiny is where true happiness really lies for me. I love my life. I am never wishing for the weekend or dreading Monday morning. Every day for me is filled with fun, love and laughter.*
>
> Kelly Murrell, Gamechanger

Seize every opportunity

> *My biggest obstacle – confidence in myself. The way I see it is if I can't even get my dogs to do what I need them to do, then what right do I have to be trying to teach others. I'm slowly getting over that. Running sessions with the local dog training club has been a very low pressure way to get experience and*

*see if it is something I can do. Because I'm not getting paid
and the classes I run are pay-on-the-night (a very small
amount to cover hall hire costs), it's a lot easier to feel that
people will get value for the time and money they spend.*

Fred Hoare, Gamechanger

Seize opportunities that are there for you. Have an opportunistic mindset, seek opportunities out, look for them and make things happen. Ok, so the opportunity for your dog business could be anything from a new venue, a partnership opportunity, an upsell (something you could package with your existing service), an opportunity of a new client base or a like-minded sponsor – the possibilities are endless. They are all right there. But listen up: you need to have your wits about you, you need to have your eyes open, you need to be ready and you can't snooze. You know the saying, you snooze you lose, and never has it been more true than when you run your own business.

Success is where preparation and opportunity meet. Prepare to say yes, prepare to be surprised and make a great decision, play the scenarios in your head. be brave, be bold, be ready. Don't miss an opportunity because it comes dressed as hard work.

*Say yes to every opportunity that comes your way. You never
know what it might lead to and just have faith that the person
who offered you the chance thinks you are capable even if
you don't at the time!*

Kate and Guy Walker-Springett, Gamechangers

Finding your place

I remember the day I walked into East Bowerland Farm. I was immediately in love: I knew it as my home. How can that be, you may ask? Well, I had replayed that moment so many hundreds of times in my head, before I ever set foot on Bowerland soil. You may think I'm crazy, but I mean it. I had been to this place many, many times in my head. I had walked all of the fields and I knew exactly how it felt, how it smelt and, most importantly, how it made me feel. Bowerlands was to be the birthplace of absoluteDogs and the lifetime home of Devon Dogs and my whole family. A very special place indeed.

Was it hard work? Yes. Is it hard work? Yes. Do I love it? Hell yeah. It is every one of my dreams all wrapped into one. The most incredible space for everything. In the end we only regret the chances we didn't take and I'm so very, very, very grateful that my family let me gamble on this one, for it has been the catalyst to the change of everything for us. To see an opportunity, we must be open and ready to all thoughts. Are you open and ready to all thoughts? I mean really ready? And sometimes we might fail, but failure is just another opportunity to get up, stand up, show up, dust off and try again.

Get ahead of the game, and stay there

I have never had any formal business coaching, but I seem to have a keen eye for business and every business I have worked within, set up myself or coached has been successful and in a big way. And one of the very first things I learned is this: first you need to get ahead, and then you need to make sure that you maintain that position and stay ahead.

It is not enough that you have built a business. You now need to work out staying in business. Your goal is to take the edge, to dare to be different, to give yourself that strategic advantage, to play your own game, to stand out from the crowd, to be at the forefront, to come up with novel concepts. You've got to bring your A game to the entrepreneurial life and you've got to keep bringing it. Always be one step further than that business with the similar business model snapping at your heels.

Your growth mindset is vital. This is a key stage, and the vital next step to being an action taker.

> *No progression is regression.*
>
> Tom Mitchell

Building your business

> *Opportunity is missed by most people because it is dressed in overalls and looks like work.*
>
> Anonymous

Building your business

This is a great time to revisit the Purposeful Action Planning Method from Chapter 9. Consider in terms of your business development:

1. What do I really want?

2. What is my purpose? What are my deep reasons? What makes this a must? What is the powerful why that drives this?

3. What needs to happen – the get-to-do list, not just one or two things but the plan?

When answering these questions, bear the following in mind:

- The who, where, what, why and when
- The premises
- The long-term plan
- The team
- The passion to mission

Get it all down on paper, draw up your action plan and to do list, and go for it. Just keep taking that next step and before you know it, you will be crushing those business goals.

Reach for the stars

Together, with Megan's help and the counselling from the Pro Dog Trainer tribe, I design my days to be positive and purposeful. I now have two days off a week, as does Megan. We support each other with weekly meetings and discuss cases, what works and what doesn't work, and, most importantly, we laugh. We enjoy each other's company and we revel in our passion of dog training together. We have a vision of greater things, a bigger training facility, hiring another trainer within the year, creatively designing new types of classes, building our local tribe of amazing students to maintain our positivity and optimism. I have discovered, through Pro Dog Trainer and absoluteDogs, that the sky is the limit when you are a unicorn.

Teri Thomas, Gamechanger

On time

Time is free, but priceless. You can't own it, but you can use it, and once it is lost you will never get it back. We spend the majority of our adult life working, yet over 50% of us want to leave our jobs because we don't enjoy them. You can get more money, but you can never get more time.

Value your time

Your time is limited, so don't waste it living someone else's life. The bad news is time flies; the good news is you are the pilot. You get a new 86,400 seconds every single day, and you will never make them up again. We think that it's people wasting our time when it's really us giving them permission to do that.

Some of us lose the people most important to us because we don't value their time. Sometimes we don't recognise how important someone is until it's too late.

Value your time like it is the most precious thing you possess – because it is.

Record it

Your ability to manage your time is one of the key skills that will determine your success as an entrepreneur. You must have the ability to manage the various competing demands on your time as a business owner. If you don't, you will become directionless, swamped and be blown about like an empty crisp packet in the wind.

Modern life is busy. Business life is even more crazy. If you are really struggling to know where your time goes, keep a time record for two weeks. Note everything down and be 100% honest. No one needs to read it but you, but it will help you discover where your time goes, what your time sinks are, whether you are doing what you think you are doing, and work out how you could spend your time more appropriately.

Push it

Peter Thiel says, "If you have a ten year plan of how to get somewhere; you should ask yourself why can't you do it in six months?"

You have the ability to renegotiate your reality for sure – it just takes a bit of self-belief and some practice. It is all very possible.

Love it

The greatest time of your life really and truly is right now. Right in this moment. Right here.

If you don't appreciate the moment that you are in right now, some day you will look back and in the blink of an eye it will be gone. I still feel like I'm 16. In fact, I can't quite believe I'm not. It doesn't seem real. Now, that doesn't mean that today is perfect, but it is real and it is now.

You will spend your life waiting for the next thing, looking towards the future, always excited about tomorrow. The future is us just making fake movies in our head that don't exist. The greatest moment is right here, and right now. If you look forwards or backwards you are missing what's right in front of you. We are putting off our happiness until someday, and when is someday? It is no day. Your time is now – enjoy it.

> *First step, be accountable. Second step, make it work. Third step, just hold on and enjoy the ride.*
>
> Becky Beacock, Gamechanger

CHAPTER 12

THE FIRST STEP TOWARDS YOUR NEW LIFE

Become a Gamechanger

> *The only way to do great work is to love what you do. If you haven't found it yet, keep looking. Don't settle.*
>
> Steve Jobs

Do you feel it? The daydreams, the spark, that whispered voice, that feeling that there is something else out there for you, the hope that the life you dream of could be yours? That's your soul calling and it is telling you that it is time. It is time to change. It is time to fly. It is time to be you.

Make the choices that are right for *you*! Sometimes it will be really hard; sometimes it will be easy. If passion is at the heart of your mission, and what you are doing sets your soul on fire, then you will always find a way. Ask questions, dig deep, explore what's out there. The world is waiting!

Are you ready to take action? Ready to step into a future where you live your true life? With dazzling tomorrows for yourself, your dogs and those you could help with your skills? Be brave, risk moving forward, and step into the light of a life lived on purpose, with intention, with motivation and with joy.

Are you ready to become a Gamechanger?

> *Our deepest fear is that we are powerful beyond measure. It is our light, not our darkness, that most frightens us. Your playing small does not serve the world. There is nothing enlightened about shrinking so that other people won't feel insecure around you.*
>
> Marianne Williamson

Join the Pro Dog Trainer tribe

No person is an island. When setting out on a journey of incredible life change, it helps to know that there is a safe place you can go for advice and support, where a group of like-minded individuals wait with expert knowledge, advice and support, ready to help and cheer every step you take.

Who are these people, I hear you ask? These are the solution seeking, game changing members of the absoluteDogs Pro Dog Trainer tribe.

The dog training world can sometimes feel like a pretty lonely and competitive place. In the Pro Dog Trainer tribe you will find a unique group of trainers who deliver cutting-edge, innovative training and who work together to improve the world of dog training. From those just starting out with their own dogs through to those with many years of experience in running their own dog based business, there is a wide and varied base of skills and knowledge within the group, and everyone is willing to share. This is a group where you can let your soul shine, and learn and grow in a safe and supportive environment.

Ready to be the true you? Join us here and get ready to fly: prodogtrainer.me

> *The minute you choose to do what you really want to do, it's a different kind of life.*
>
> Buckminster Fuller

Gamechanger testimonials

> *The positivity in the Pro Dog Trainer tribe was like nothing I had ever encountered before. Everyone was happy, helpful and supportive of each other. The life lessons provided by Tom and Lauren, the enthusiasm and positivity throughout the group and, oh yes, the massive amount of dog training knowledge led me to the decision that I was going to retire from my 'human' career and become a full-time dog trainer.*
>
> Janine Vander Yacht

> *I have discovered, through Pro Dog Trainer and absoluteDogs that the sky is the limit when you are a unicorn. The moral of my life story is to be an action taker.*
> *In one short year from risking it and following Pro Dog Trainer, my life has made a complete 180. My married life is*

richer, my business life is successful beyond my wildest dreams and my personal life is fulfilled. Be brave, have grit, build tolerance of frustration, be confident, be optimistic, be flexible. All the things we teach our students are all the things we learn along the way too. We are all connected.

Teri Thomas

Pro Dog Trainer has given me confidence and belief in myself. It has given me back my sense of me and my passion and enthusiasm for what I love to do. Being a Gamechanger means following my intuition, trusting in my abilities to make a positive change in the life of dogs through spreading the knowledge of training with kindness. Pro Dog Trainer can be summed up in these words: fun, support, sharing, inspiring, transforming, confidence, flexibility, enthusiasm, optimism, laughter, for the love of dogs.

Sarah Jane McLaren

Both Pro Trainer and absoluteDogs have helped immensely. I honestly don't think we would be where we are today if it wasn't for being part of this community – From being a source of knowledge and expertise, both in terms of dog-specific knowledge and ideas, but also as a source of inspiration from other people's journeys and the feeling that we were not alone in this.

Kate and Guy Walker-Springett

absoluteDogs and Pro Dog Trainer have transformed my life. They've given me the confidence in myself I needed to move forward and step boldly in the direction of my dreams. I've gone from being extremely shy and unsure of myself to being an action taking, solution seeking optimist who owns her talents and puts them out there into the world. I'm part of the absoluteDogs team now and I'm so grateful for the opportunities that have come my way through absoluteDogs and Pro Dog Trainer. Thank you, Lauren and Tom. Here's to the Gamechangers!

Nicola Cameron